Harry Belafonte Autobiography

Sir Gardner Bourn

Contents

Chapter 1

My New York City Apartment Phone Rang Really Late At Night. August 4th, 1964 Was A Night. For Those Of Us Involved In The Civil Rights Struggle, But Particularly For Those In Mississippi, This Was A Night Of Sorrow And Fury. It's A Crisis Situation Down Here, The Young Guy On The Call Stated. "Please Assist Us."

Hundreds Of Volunteers, Mostly Students From Northern Institutions, Many Of Them White, All Of Them Understanding How Risky The Task Would Be, Had Traveled South To Register Black Voters And Help Rural Blacks In Pursuit Of Their Civil Rights At The Beginning Of That Tragic Summer. Spread Out Throughout The Front Lines Of The Civil Rights Movement, They Were Defenseless Against The Raging Segregationists.

The Cops In Mississippi Were Ready To Beat Them Bloody And Put Them In Prison At A Moment's Notice. It's Possible That The Kkk Might Fare Much Worse. That Day, We Realized How Much Worse Things Might Become. Three Missing Volunteers Were Discovered Dead In A Small Burial Close To Philadelphia, Mississippi On June 21. Michael Schwerner, James Chaney, And Andrew Goodman (Two White Men And One Black Man) Were Ambushed By The Ku Klux Klan After Being Caught For A Traffic Infraction, Held For A Short Time, And Then Released. Each Victim Had Been Beaten Before Being Shot. The Black Volunteer Chaney Was Mutilated And Tormented.

I Had Been Instrumental In Getting The Ball Rolling Financially For Mississippi Freedom Summer. I Had Reached Out To All The Famous Musicians I Knew For Help, Including Frank Sinatra, Lena Horne, Henry Fonda, Marlon Brando, Joan Baez, The Kingston Trio, Dick

Gregory, And Many More. Lots Of Groceries, Petrol, And Groceries Were Purchased With That Money. Now, Though, More Was Required. More Than That, Really. The Initial Schedule Saw Students Working In Two-Week Periods Before Returning Home And Being Replaced. Every Shift Had Insisted On Sticking Despite The Ominous Disappearance Of Schwerner, Chaney, And Goodman. After The Remains Were Discovered, The Volunteers Decided To Extend Their Stay Into The Autumn. "It's Good That They're Staying," The Young Guy Who Phoned Me That Night, Jim Forman, Said To Me. Among The Many Civil Rights Organizations Operating In The Region, The Student Nonviolent Coordinating Committee (Sncc) Operated Under Jim's Effective Leadership. If They Leave Now, Or Even At The End Of August, The Klan Will Claim It Frightened Them Into Leaving, And The Media Will Report It As Such. We Can Register Thousands More Voters If They All Remain. We Just Don't Have The Means To Support Their Continued Presence Here.

I Enquired, "What Do You Need?"

"A Minimum Of Fifty Grand."

I Assured Him That I Would Find A Way To Obtain It. Asking, "How Soon Do You Need It?"

The Remaining Funds Will Be Spent In Less Than 72 Hours.

Forman Had One More Item To Tell Me Before He Hung Up The Phone. He Said, "This Could Get Really Ugly." Many Individuals Are Now Expressing The View That 'Enough Is Enough' And That Nonviolence Should Be Abandoned. Guns Are Being Taken Up By Them. I'm Afraid They'll Decide To Solve The Problem On Their Own.

I Gave A Lot Of Thought To How I Might Get The Money To Greenwood, Mississippi And Where It May Come From. I Had Previously Donated To Sncc In Its Formative Years With A Check For A Sum Not Much Lower Than That, And I Had The Resources To Cover The Whole $50,000. In My Case, "Anything Goes," Yet I Had A Responsibility To Provide For My Loved Ones Financially. In The Late 1940s, When Paul Robeson Was Blacklisted As A Communist, He Had Given So Much Money To Social Causes That He Left Himself Vulnerable To His Enemies, Chief Among Them The Federal Government, A Formidable Force Led By J. Edgar Hoover And The Federal Bureau Of Investigation. Carnegie Hall And Other American Venues Had Been Intimidated Into Not Employing Him By Senator Joseph Mccarthy, And The Federal Government Had Stolen His Passport To Prevent Him From Playing Overseas And Making A Livelihood. Paul Exhausted His Funds And Fell Into A Severe Depression As A Result. Never Will I Forget It. For The Most Part, I'd Have To Find Other People To Help Me Fund This. In Two At The Most Three Days. The Question Of How To Transfer The Funds To Mississippi Also Arose. A Black Civil Rights Activist Couldn't Go Go To His Local Western Union And Ask For $50,000, Therefore I Couldn't Wire It To Him. A Mile Of Driving Wouldn't Get Him Out Of Danger. A White Student Volunteer Would Do The Same. When It Comes To Banks, Don't You Just Love How They're All Owned And Run By The White Elite Of Mississippi? No Way.

The Funds Could Only Be Brought In By Cash Transfer. And Unless I Can Think Of A Better Plan, I'll Have To Dismantle It By Hand.

My New York City-Based Wife, Julie, Initiated The Planning Stages Of A Fund-Raiser At Our West End

Avenue Apartment. I Took A Plane To The Windy City. Irv Kupcinet, A Journalist Who Is As Influential In His Hometown As Walter Winchell Was In New York, Invited Scores Of People To His House With Just Two Days' Notice. Cash-Wielding White Visitors. As A Black Artist, Why Did I Have So Much Influence On Irv And His Pals? My Early Years As A Troubadour On The Club Circuit In The '50s Were The Origin Of Our Friendship, But That's Just Half Of The Tale. I Don't Know How I Did It, But I Was Able To Reach Over The Racial Gap And Offer A Helping Hand. That Was As Much About The Present As It Was About Me, I Realized. As If I Were The Personal Representative Of The Civil Rights Movement, Irv's Guests, Galvanized By The Horrifying News Of The Volunteers' Killings, Threw Cash And Checks At Me Totaling $35,000. Which I Suppose I Was, Kind Of, In That Room, On That Night. My Vacation To Montreal Netted Me An Extra $20,000. When I Came Back To New York, Julie And I Had A Fundraiser At Our Apartment And Raised An Additional $15,000. I Needed To Raise $100,000 But Only Had Time To Collect $70,000. When I Saw That Number, I Couldn't Help But Feel Satisfied. Now That I Was Traveling With Sidney Poitier, A Friend Of Mine From When We Were Both Struggling Performers In Harlem, I Felt Even Better About The Whole Thing.

I Considered Sidney A Brother. We Were Both Born In The Caribbean And Both Had A Strong Drive To Escape Our Families' Abject Poverty. We Were Both Successful Performers, Which Was Unbelievable. Sidney Was The Most Famous Black Actor In The Industry. My Early Career Was Spent As A Singer, But I Eventually Achieved Success On Broadway And In Hollywood As Well. To Put It Plainly, We Were The Two Greatest Black Male

Performers In The World. We Had Our Political And Personal Disagreements, But We Also Competed Like Brothers. Sidney, To Begin With, Exhibited A Greater Degree Of Caution Than I Did. When I Invited Him To Come With Me, He Questioned Cautiously, "What Kind Of Protection Are You Going To Have?"

"Bobby And I Discussed It," I Replied. After The Killing Of His Brother, President Johnson Allowed Robert F. Kennedy To Continue In His Role As U.S. Attorney General. He Sent Me To Burke Marshall, Who Is In Charge Of The Civil Rights Section At The Department Of Justice. Both Of Them Were Aware Of The Danger I Was In. The Likelihood Of A Klansman Firing A Shot At Me Was Considerable In The Hostile Environment Of Mississippi. Defeating The New York-Based, Affluent, Black Singer Who Assumed He Understood What Was Best For The South And Who Was Thus Knocked Off? You Get Ten! On The Phone, Marshall Listened To My Plans And Made Notes. I Told Sidney Everything That Had Happened, Assuming Maybe Too Much Based On My Talk With Marshall. Marshall Is Working On It, I Assured Him. In Other Words, "There Will Be Federal Security Checks At Every Stage."

All The Way, As Sidney Repeated.

To Which She Responded, "Right," On My Part. It Will Be More Challenging For Them To Eliminate Two Black Stars Than Than One. There's Safety In Numbers, Dude.

The Glumly Accepting "Okay," Said By Sidney. "But What About After This, Harry?"

"Yeah?"

To Which The Respondent Emphatically Said, "Never Call Me Again."

I Knew Sidney Well Enough At The Time To Realize He Was Serious. Of Course, I Decided To Take His Anger In

Stride And Have A Good Chuckle About It, But I Was The Only One Who Did. We Boarded An Aircraft In Newark, New Jersey, Headed For Jackson, Mississippi, With No One Else On Board And Very Little Talk. Since I Had Cashed The Cheques From The Fundraisers, We Now Had $70,000 In Banknotes Of Various Denominations Jammed Inside A Black Medical Bag. Back In Those Distant Days, Nobody Seemed To Care What We Were Toting About. Someone From The Crew Just Waved Us On.

We Were The Final Aircraft Of The Day Into Jackson's Major Airport. Jim Forman And Two Other Sncc Volunteers Were Waiting For Us At The Terminal, But Other From Us, There Was No One Else There. A Black Maintenance Worker With A Broom Was The Sole Representative Of Local Government We Saw. Sidney Gave Me An Irritated Look. How About That For National Defense?

"Probably An Fbi Agent In Disguise," I Said. Sidney Didn't Even Crack A Smile.

A Tiny Cessna Was Waiting For Us On A Private Runway Near The Airport, And The Volunteers Escorted Us There Through The Thick, Muggy Night In Mississippi. The White Pilot Welcomed Us Gravely With A Thick Southern Drawl. I Sneaked A Glance At Him As We All Climbed In Together. Were We Being Led Into A Trap By A Klansman? He Looked Like He Belonged In The Part.

As The Little Aircraft Got Closer And Closer To Greenwood, My Worries Increased. The Journey Was Not Smooth. Apparently, The Pilot Was Indifferent. Every Dip Of The Aircraft Seemed Like The Beginning Of The End To Us.

At Last, We Touched Down On A Dirt Runway Next To A Shed That Served As The Airport For Greenwood. The

Pilot Circled Around In Front Of It, Let Us Out, And Then Flew Off Without Waiting. For Our Part, We're Curious As To What He Knew That We Didn't. The Heat And The Darkness Both Hit Me At Once As I Glanced About. No Night Has Ever Been So Dark Before. In That Moment, I Found Myself Thinking Of "The Creation," A Poem Written By James Weldon Johnson.

Blacker Than A Hundred Midnights, Darkness Engulfed All Of Creation As Far As The Lord's Sight Could See.

In The Depths Of A Cypress Swamp.

When I Came Back To New York, Julie And I Had A Fundraiser At Our Apartment And Raised An Additional $15,000. I Needed To Raise $100,000 But Only Had Time To Collect $70,000. When I Saw That Number, I Couldn't Help But Feel Satisfied. When I Saw That Two Additional Sncc Volunteers, Along With Two Automobiles, Were Waiting For Us, I Immediately Felt Better. There Were Two Cars, And Sidney And I Hopped Into The Rear Of The First One, With Jim Forman In The Passenger Seat And A Young Snccer Called Willie Blue Behind The Wheel. Both Vehicles Were Sandblasted Down To A Matte Finish So They Wouldn't Reflect Light At Night. An Appropriate Safety Measure That Falls Short: Willie And The Other Driver Began Their Vehicles, And At The Other End Of The Pitch-Black Airstrip, A Long Line Of Headlights Flashed On. My First Thought Was, "That Must Be The Federal Agents," And I Told Sidney The Same Thing. However, We Could Make Out That The Two Sets Of Headlights Were Mounted At Varying Heights And Shone With Varying Intensities. My Dreams Were Smashed By Willie Blue. As He Said, "Agents, My Ass," We May Infer That He Was Addressing The Agents. Say It With Me Now: "That's The Klan."

Willie And The Other Driver Turned Around And Began Racing Toward The Line Of Headlights Instead Than Away From Them, In The Direction Of The Major Route Into Town. We Were Able To Get Near Enough To Make Out The Vague Silhouettes Of A Handful Of Rusty Pickups. Then, At What Seemed To Be A Signal, Willie And The Other Driver Suddenly Turned Off The Main Road And Into A Rougher Side Path Leading Towards Town. Behind Us, A Queue Of Trucks Formed.

I Yelled To The Driver, "Why Aren't You Driving Faster?" Willie Was Driving Exactly Forty Miles Per Hour. As The Saying Goes, "Faster, Man!"

"No!" Yelled Replied Willie. That's The Plan All Along, You See. Someone Called Up A State Policeman Who Was Waiting In His Cruiser With The Lights Off To Pull Us Up For Speeding. He Drives Us To The Station, Where We Are Released An Hour Later To Find Additional Klan Members Waiting For Us. That's The Way They Function. That's How Those Young Men Were Slaughtered.

The First Pickup Vehicle Came Up Quickly Behind Us And Began Passing. The Two-By-Four Across The Grille Served As An Improvised Battering Ram, And There Was No License Plate Visible Through The Back Window. To Prevent The Truck From Passing, Willie Veered Into The Midst Of The Two Lanes Of Traffic. Now The Truck Was Slamming Into Our Automobile From Behind. There's No Way We Can Have Willie Drive Up Next To Us, Willie Yelled. Threateningly, "They'll Shoot."

Willie Turned On His Two-Way Radio And Spoke With The Sncc Headquarters In Greenwood. There Was A Crackling Voice On The Other End Of The Walkie-Talkie, Saying, "We're On Our Way."

Willie Stubbornly Refused To Veer To The Left Whenever The Pickup Vehicle Attempted To Pass Us And Instead

Remained In The Middle Of The Road. After What Felt Like Two Or Three Scary Minutes, I Peered Down The Road And Saw A Line Of Automobiles Approaching Us From Greenwood. "That's Them," Willie Identified. To Save The Day, The Sncc Team Has Arrived. Even Though My Heart Was Still Racing, I Began To Take Deep Breaths Again.

The Pickup Trucks Stopped Moving And Their Beams Dimmed As The Column Of Vehicles Neared. A Dozen Or More Gunfire Rang Out At That Time. We Couldn't Determine Whether The Klansmen Were Shooting At Us Or At Nothing In Particular. Our Vehicles Were Not Struck By Gunfire, And Nobody Was Injured. We Were Safe Amid The Sncc Fleet When We Heard More Gunfire Behind Us And Decided To Take A Detour Off The Main Route.

Through Greenwood And Beyond, The Convoy Brought Us To An Elks Hall Filled With Hundreds Of Volunteers. They Had Spent The Whole Day Debating Their Next Course Of Action, And They Were All Stressed Out And Exhausted. They Had Few Real Choices Other From Ours. The Throng Cheered As Sidney And I Entered The Building. Sidney And I Had Heard Our Fair Share Of Cheers In Our Time, But Nothing Like That. These Volunteers Were Emotionally And Physically Drained After Weeks Of Dangerous, Isolating Fieldwork. It Meant A Lot To Them, And To Us, That Two Of The Biggest Black Stars In The World Would Step In To Express Unity With Them.

The Gathering Began Singing A Spiritual That Had Provided Daily Solace And Inspiration To These Courageous Volunteers, And Then Another One About Freedom. Silence Prevailed Until Sidney Finally Broke It. Saying, "I Am Thirty-Seven Years Old," He Informed The

Audience Of His Age. This Room May Be Full Of Affection, Yet "I Have Been A Lonely Man All My Life" Is A Lie. Then Sidney Faced Me Directly. I Waited Till Silence Had Settled, Then I Sung, "Day-O..." A Shout From The Audience Took Over. The "Banana Boat Song" Was My Distinctive Tune, But It Was Also The Anthem Of The Working Poor, A Song Of Exhaustion And Optimism That Spoke Directly To The Emotions Of The Volunteers That Night. The Lyrics "Freedom, Freedom, Freedom Come And It Won't Be Long" Were Adapted From The Folk Song "Day-O, Day-O / Daylight Come And I Want To Go Home" By The Civil Rights Movement. After The Two Rounds Of Singing Were Over, I Held Up The Black Bag I Had Brought, Flipped It On The Table In Front Of Me, And Let The Bundles Of Cash Tumble Out To Frenzied Cheers.

Sidney Was Right; There Was A Lot Of Affection In That Barn. But Outside, Idle Automobiles Belonged To Ku Klux Klan Members; We Barely Managed To Keep Them Out Of Greenwood. Aerial Kkk Fliers Urging Mississippians To Stand Up To "The Niggers" And Protect Their Rights Had Been Dropped That Day. After Eating Chicken And Spareribs That Evening, Sidney And I Were Brought To The Residence Where We Would Spend The Night As Armed Guards Stood Watch Outside. Under The Window In Our Bedroom Was A Double Bed That Wasn't Too Squished Up Against The Wall. Sidney's Face Became White At This.

At For This Journey, I Was Accompanied By Sidney Poitier, A Friend From Our Days Spent As Struggling Performers In Harlem.

I Considered Sidney A Brother. We Were Both Born In The Caribbean And Both Had A Strong Drive To Escape Our Families' Abject Poverty. We Were Both Successful

Performers, Which Was Unbelievable. Sidney Was The Most Famous Black Actor In The Industry. My Early Career Was Spent As A Singer, But I Eventually Achieved Success On Broadway And In Hollywood As Well. To Put It Plainly, We Were The Two Greatest Black Male Performers In The World. We Had Our Political And Personal Disagreements, But We Also Competed Like Brothers. Sidney, To Begin With, Exhibited A Greater Degree Of Caution Than I Did. When I Invited Him To Come With Me, He Questioned Cautiously, "What Kind Of Protection Are You Going To Have?"

"Bobby And I Discussed It," I Replied. After The Killing Of His Brother, President Johnson Allowed Robert F. Kennedy To Continue In His Role As U.S. Attorney General. He Sent Me To Burke Marshall, Who Is In Charge Of The Civil Rights Section At The Department Of Justice. Both Of Them Were Aware Of The Danger I Was In. The Likelihood Of A Klansman Firing A Shot At Me Was Considerable In The Hostile Environment Of Mississippi. Defeating The New York-Based, Affluent, Black Singer Who Assumed He Understood What Was Best For The South And Who Was Thus Knocked Off? You Get Ten! On The Phone, Marshall Listened To My Plans And Made Notes. I Told Sidney Everything That Had Happened, Assuming Maybe Too Much Based On My Talk With Marshall. Marshall Is Working On It, I Assured Him. In Other Words, "There Will Be Federal Security Checks At Every Stage."

All The Way, As Sidney Repeated.

To Which She Responded, "Right," On My Part. It Will Be More Challenging For Them To Eliminate Two Black Stars Than Than One. There's Safety In Numbers, Dude.

The Glumly Accepting "Okay," Said By Sidney. "But What About After This, Harry?"

"Yeah?"

To Which The Respondent Emphatically Said, "Never Call Me Again."

I Knew Sidney Well Enough At The Time To Realize He Was Serious. Of Course, I Decided To Take His Anger In Stride And Have A Good Chuckle About It, But I Was The Only One Who Did. We Boarded An Aircraft In Newark, New Jersey, Headed For Jackson, Mississippi, With No One Else On Board And Very Little Talk. Since I Had Cashed The Cheques From The Fundraisers, We Now Had $70,000 In Banknotes Of Various Denominations Jammed Inside A Black Medical Bag. Back In Those Distant Days, Nobody Seemed To Care What We Were Toting About. Someone From The Crew Just Waved Us On.

We Were The Final Aircraft Of The Day Into Jackson's Major Airport. Jim Forman And Two Other Sncc Volunteers Were Waiting For Us At The Terminal, But Other From Us, There Was No One Else There. A Black Maintenance Worker With A Broom Was The Sole Representative Of Local Government We Saw. Sidney Gave Me An Irritated Look. How About That For National Defense?

"Probably An Fbi Agent In Disguise," I Said. Sidney Didn't Even Crack A Smile.

A Tiny Cessna Was Waiting For Us On A Private Runway Near The Airport, And The Volunteers Escorted Us There Through The Thick, Muggy Night In Mississippi. The White Pilot Welcomed Us Gravely With A Thick Southern Drawl. I Sneaked A Glance At Him As We All Climbed In Together. Were We Being Led Into A Trap By A Klansman? He Looked Like He Belonged In The Part.

As The Little Aircraft Got Closer And Closer To Greenwood, My Worries Increased. The Journey Was

Not Smooth. Apparently, The Pilot Was Indifferent. Every Dip Of The Aircraft Seemed Like The Beginning Of The End To Us.

At Last, We Touched Down On A Dirt Runway Next To A Shed That Served As The Airport For Greenwood. The Pilot Circled Around In Front Of It, Let Us Out, And Then Flew Off Without Waiting. For Our Part, We're Curious As To What He Knew That We Didn't. The Heat And The Darkness Both Hit Me At Once As I Glanced About. No Night Has Ever Been So Dark Before. In That Moment, I Found Myself Thinking Of "The Creation," A Poem Written By James Weldon Johnson.

Down In A Cypress Swamp, It Was Darker Than A Hundred Midnights, As Far As The Eye Of God Could See. To Which She Said, "Look, I'll Take The Inside, Okay?" I Explained That I Meant The Side Closest To The Wall. It Was Intended As An Apology; I Knew I'd Be The One Having To Squeeze In Next To My Snoring Partner.

Sidney Looked At Me With Suspicion. Yes, But If Someone Shoots Through That Window, I'll Have A Greater Chance Of Being Injured.

He Was Kind Of Kidding About It.

"Okay, Okay, I'll Take The Outside," I Finally Said.

The Idea Had Crossed Sidney's Mind. Maybe The Outside Was The Better Side If I Was Prepared To Accept It. As For Me, I'll Choose The Outside," He Answered Flatly. To Paraphrase, "If You Get Shot, I'd Hate To Have To Climb Over Your Dead Ass To Get To The Door."

We Spent Some Time Chatting In The Dark While Lying In Bed. Some Of My Ghost Tales Were Shared With Sidney. After A While, I Managed To Go Into A Fitful Slumber, Only To Be Startled Up By A Peculiar Rasping Sound In The Total Darkness. Sidney Wasn't Moving, So I Leaned Over And Gave Him A Little Prod. Nothing Was On The

Vacant Side Of The Bed. It Was Easier To Hear The Rasping. "Sidney?"

A Raspy "Yes," From Him.

Asking, "What The Fuck Are You Doing?"

"Push-Ups," Sidney Chimed In. I'm Wide Awake. And When Those Motherfuckers Come For Us, You Can Bet Your Last Dollar That I Will Be Prepared.

After Returning Home To My Family, I Sometimes Questioned My Decision To Make The Civil Rights Movement My Personal Struggle. I Understood Why I Had Gotten Engaged In The First Place; By The Summer Of 1964, Each Black American With A Beating Heart And A Moral Compass Had Done The Same, If Only By Sending In The Odd Check. Numerous White Americans Had Done So As Well. We All Knew This Was The Moment When Everything Would Change. More Lynchings And Beatings Would Be Intolerable. We Could Not Stand To See Any More "Whites Only" Signs Up In The Segregated South's Hotels, Restaurants, Gas Stations, Water Fountains, And Bus Stops. We Couldn't Stand By And Watch Black Americans Be Treated Like Slaves Again. That Was Common Knowledge. When I Heard Images On The News Of Student Demonstrators Being Thrashed With Truncheons By State Police And Bitten By Police Attack Dogs, I Felt Personally Insulted, But Why? I Was Sitting In My Twenty-One-Room Apartment On West End Avenue. From The President To The Fbi To The Military To The Average Person On The Street, What Source Of Anger Did Those Images Tap Into, And Why Had I Felt Angry, For So Long, About So Many Other Issues Of Freedom, Democracy, And Equality? How Could I Have Possibly Harmed The Career Trajectory That Had Made Me, At The Age Of Thirty, The

World's First So-Called Black Matinee Idol, When I Cared So Much About Succeeding As An Actor And Singer?

The Majority Of The Credit Goes To My Mom. My Dad Was In There, Too, But To A Lesser Extent. I Was Aware Even At A Young Age That I Was A Cultural Misfit, Caught Between Two Worlds: The West Indian And The American. And I Was Dirt Poor In Kingston And Harlem, The Two Real Worlds I'd Straddled As A Youngster. I Felt A Lot Of Frustration Because Of It.

Even After Being Deeply Involved In The Civil Rights Movement, I Would Still Be Struggling To Comprehend And Dissipate That Rage. I Would Take Martin Luther King, Jr. As My Inspiration And Adopt Nonviolence Not Only As A Strategy For Social Change But As A Way Of Life. Fifty Years Of Freudian Analysis May Be Useful As Well. But Even As I Started Writing Out My Life's Tale, I Was Still Putting The Pieces Together. After Reading This Book, I Have Gained Knowledge. I See The Complicated, Angry, Wounded, And Usually Alone Young Kid That I Once Was. But I'm Not Sure Why This Particular Young Child Would Use His Rage To Elevate Himself, Gain Notoriety, And Ultimately Make It His Goal To Destroy Racial Boundaries And Injustice With Such Grim Resolve.

Perhaps What Matters More Is What You Do With Your Anger Rather Than Its Origin.

Chapter 2

Because Of My Family's Financial Situation, I Assumed That Being Poor Would Always Be My Default State Of Being. It Shaped Who I Was And, Deep Down, I Believe It Still Does. I Was Furious, Sure, But Also Scared And Exposed. When My Mother Disembarked From A Boat Named The Cananova At Ellis Island On July 20, 1926, She Experienced All Of These Emotions As Well. There Was Initial Optimism, However.

My Mother, Melvine Love, Was A Real Jamaican Beauty When She Was Twenty-One Years Old. She Had Dark Eyes, High Cheekbones, And A Slim Figure That She Carried With Such Pride And Purpose That It Was Impossible To Miss Her Confidence. She Was Born Into A Farming Family In The Highlands Of St. Ann Parish, On The Island's North Shore, And Was One Of Thirteen Children. Her Café Au Lait Complexion Was A Giveaway That She Was Of Mixed Race. Her Mother Was The White Daughter Of A Scottish Father Who Had Moved His Family To Jamaica To Manage A Farm For An Absentee Owner; Her Father Was A Black Sharecropper. It Was A Familiar Tale Among Islanders. Large Families Were Also Common, And Children Did Not Always Come From The Same Set Of Parents. I'm Quite Sure My Grandpa Had A Few Children, And I'm Very Sure That A Couple Of My Mother's Siblings Had Darker Or Lighter Complexion Because Of That. My Mom, Millie, Was The Only Girl In A Family Of 10 To Make It Through Childhood. Four Of Millie's Siblings Had Already Arrived In New York; Two Were Waiting For Her In The Lobby As They Had Abandoned Jamaica For The Hardships Of Farming. Aunt Liz Wore A Stylish Hat And A Well-Fitting Wool Suit. The Costume Served Its Purpose Well, As

Intended. My Uncle Castel, Who Was With Her, Looked Just Like The Driver; In Fact, He Drove A Taxi And Picked Up Harlem Customers Who No Respectable White Cab Driver Would Touch Since They Never Drove To Harlem. Millie, Who Had Grown Up In A Two-Room Hut In Rural Jamaica, Clung To Liz's Elbow As She Took Her First Steps In Manhattan, Awestruck By The Throngs Of People And The Honking Of Cars. Incredible Shock And Awe. However, It Was Too Late To Turn Back. If Millie Ever Had Any Concerns About Coming, She Need Just Think Back To The Reason She Came. She Had Learnt To Read And Write On A Slate Board With The Aid Of Her Mother And Entertained The Possibility That She May One Day Attend College. She Had Displayed The Slate To Her Father With Pride When She Was Eight Years Old, Her Heart Full Of Hopes And Dreams. Okay, That's All You Need, Her Dad Had Said. You May Now Spend Your Mornings Instructing Your Younger Sibling To Reach Your Level Of Proficiency And Your Afternoons Helping Out In The Fields. An Education? What Was She Thinking? The Beautiful Curves And Strokes Of My Mother's Handwriting Were All That Remained Of Her Girlhood Ambitions To Me All Those Years Afterwards.

After Hailing Her First Cab, Millie Found Herself In Harlem's West Indian Neighborhood At The Corner Of 145th Street And Seventh Avenue. Liz's Building Was Among The Nicest On The Street. A Neighbor's Kind Welcome Followed Her As She Brought Her Younger Sister Inside. To Whoever It May Concern: "Hello, Miz Hines." Millie Gave Her An Inquisitive Glance But Said Nothing As They Entered The Apartment's Exquisite Six-Room Layout, Which Included Four Bedrooms. Millie Mustered The Words, "It's Beautiful." Is This The Standard Of Living For All Of New York City? Liz Said That

Three Of The Four Bedrooms Were Rented Out, And That The Rent Was Split Between Them. She Had Sacrificed Financially By Making One Of The Bedrooms Accessible To Millie, As Liz Pointed Out Was Unnecessary. Liz Told Millie She Could Remain In The Apartment While She Got Things Rolling. Millie Understood What Liz Meant By "Until You Find A Man" From The Way She Chuckled As She Said It.

Millie Joined A Broader Immigrant Community As Its Newest Member. In Harlem In 1926, A White New Yorker Would Not Be Able To Tell The Difference Between American And Caribbean Blacks, Save For The Latter's Lilting Accents. However, The Distinctions Were Striking. Black Americans Were Forced To Endure Slavery And Segregation For A Combined 200 Years In The United States. Since They'd Been Poor For So Long, Most People Had Given Up Hope. They Had Learnt To Adapt To Its Discomforts, Yet Continued To Struggle To Get Free. Not So In Early Twentieth-Century Harlem, Where Many People From The Caribbean Lived. They Were The Children Of Immigrants, And They Were Driven To Provide A Better Life For Their Families. Their Forebears Were Slaves In Conditions That Were Often More Brutal Than Those In The American South; They Were Often Worked To Death Like Mules. However, It Was Precisely Because Of These Harsher Conditions That More Slave Rebellions And Escapes Were Attempted. Those Uprisings Helped Hasten The Abolition Of Slavery In The Colonies Of Spain, France, And England By The Middle Of The Nineteenth Century. Even When They Educated A Competent Cadre Of Civil Employees To Act As Overseers For Their Absentee Landlords, The Islanders' Defiant Nature Remained A Problem. Gradually, Blacks On The Islands Gained Freedom Until The Mid-1920s,

When They Might Hope To Become Landowners, Attorneys, And Physicians. They Also Made Up The Overwhelming Majority On Several Of The Islands. Although Most Remained Economically Impoverished, They Did Not Lack Pride Or Drive.

Many Of The People Who Eventually Settled In Harlem Began Their Journey In The Gulfport, Mississippi, Region, Where They Were Lured By The Promise Of Permanent Labor But Were Instead Forced Into Indentured Servitude. They Were Sent By Contractors To The Interior, Where They Worked Cutting Sugarcane And Picking Cotton In Exchange For Meager Wages And Slept In Squalid Barracks While Accruing Debt At The Company Shop. They Were No Less Fugitive Slaves Than Their Ancestors On The Islands, But The Hardest And Most Determined Among Them Had Fled To Journey North.

Therefore, The West Indian Community In Harlem Was Not Going To Let Anything Stand In Their Way. Not The Systemic, Hopeless Poverty That Black Americans In The United States Face. Meanwhile, Blacks In The Us Referred To The Islanders As The "Jews" Of Their Neighborhood. It Was An Anti-Semitic Slur, But There Was Some Substance To The Accusation. The Islanders, Like The Jews Who Had Colonized Other Parts Of Harlem, Placed A High Value On Education. They Had Lofty Goals, Much Like Jews. And Like Several Americans Of Jewish Descent In The Roaring Twenties, They Found Success Outside The Law If They Couldn't Make It On The Inside. During Prohibition, Many Islanders Worked As Rumrunners, Bringing The Illegal Substance From The West Indies To The East Coast. They Controlled All The Gambling Numbers In Harlem. Millie Obviously Picked It Up Early On, Since Liz And Her Sometimes-Boyfriend Jimmy Hines Operated A Numbers Business.

Not Long Previously, A Small Group Of West Indians Had Devised The Numbers Game, Introduced It To Harlem, And By The Mid-1920s Had Turned It Into A Very Lucrative But Criminal Gang. The Clarity Of The Notion Was Astounding. On Any Given Day, People Would Wager On The Last Three Digits Of A Number That Was Publicly Tallied. It Would Enough To Use The Stock Market's Closing Price. The Treasury's Funds Would Be Depleted As Well. The Sum Of The Winnings From One Track's Winning Horses That Afternoon Was The Most Talked About Statistic. When The Pennies And Dollars Were Added Together, All Of These Sums Went Above Three Digits, Thus The Gamblers Attempted To Predict The Last Three Numbers At Random. The "Full Number" Would Be 464 If The Daily Payout For A Complete Card Of Winners Was $264.64. The Chances Of Correctly Guessing All Three In Sequence Were One In A Thousand. For A Much Smaller Payout, You May Wager On A Single Digit Or Even A Pair Of Digits, Such As The Initial Number Or The First Two.

Liz Was A Numbers Operator, Therefore She Ran Her Own Bank And Accepted Wagers From Customers For Many Blocks. Her Morning Joggers' Routine Always Included A Full Round Of The Block, With A Knock On Every House. Inquiring Minds Want To Know, "What Are You Playing Today, Mrs. Davis?" "Give Me 341 For A Quarter," He Said. Due Of The Low Entry Barrier, Almost Everyone Participated. Also, Everyone Had Their Own Personal "Dream Book" Dictionary Where Numbers Were Added Next To Key Words. The Night Before, Mrs. Davis Had A Dream About Fire, And In Her Dream Book, The Definition Of Fire Included The Numbers 341. What Kept The Game Going Was That Eventually Someone Would Win, And The Bankers Like Liz Would Pay Up.

That, And The Bankers Must Be Completely Trustworthy; If A Runner Were Detected Pocketing Bets, He Or She Would Be Severely Punished. Nothing Could Stop Mrs. Davis And Her Neighbors From Wagering As Long As They Remained Honest. And There Was Enough Left Over, Which Is Why Liz Could Afford The Expensive Apartment And Well-Tailored Wardrobe She Did.

It Would Be Impossible For Liz To Manage A Gambling Operation Solely Based On Statistics. She Needed A Strong Ally With Influence In High Places. She Relied On Jimmy Hines, Who, To Millie's Surprise, Was Not A Native Of The Islands, To Help Her With This. He Was A Corrupt Official In Mayor Jimmy Walker's Administration And A Member Of The Irish Political Party Tammany Hall. Hines Combined A Pleasant Demeanor With A Cold, Calculated Demeanor. Beginning At His Father's Stable, Where He Shoed The City's Police And Fire Horses, He Worked His Way Up The Political Ladder. It Wasn't Long Before He Was Promoted To Captain Of His District. In 1926, He Was Already Involved In Several Fields. His Numbers Operation With Liz Was Just One Of Many; He Also Extorted $30,000 Annually From Other Numbers Bosses In The Form Of Protection Money And Bribes To The Local Police. Hines's Family Included A Wife And Three Young Boys. But He Had Liz To Help Him Out On His Uptown Rounds.

Almost Every Single Sunday Night, Jimmy And "Miz Hines" Had A Rowdy Dinner Party. At Liz's Caribbean Cuisine Party, Politicians Openly Mingled With Numbers Bosses And Other Underworld Figures. Dutch Schultz, The So-Called Beer Baron, Ran The Harlem Beer Industry During Prohibition, And His Companion Lucky Luciano Were Frequent Customers. White Gangsters In The 1920s Considered The Numbers Game To Be A Waste Of

Time And Money Compared To The Other Rackets They Were Operating. The End Of Prohibition And The Great Depression Would Alter All Of That. For The Time Being, The Gangsters Were Happy To Host Their New Friends, The Numbers Operators, At Miz Hines' And Even Provided Free Drinks. Everyone Started To Let Their Guard Down As The Drinks Kept Coming. Liz Did Just That When She Introduced Millie To Eligible Bachelor Harold Bellanfanti At One Of The Sunday Meals.

Like Millie, Harold Was A Jamaican Kid Of A Mixed-Race Couple. His Mother Was A Black Jamaican, And His Father Was A White Dutch Jew Who Had Ended Up In The Islands After Striking Out In His Search For Riches And Diamonds In The West African Colonies. He Came From The Same Humble Beginnings As Millie, But Now Harold Was Carving Himself A Successful Career As A Chef On The United Fruit Company Ships (Also Known As "Banana Boats") Plying The Waters Between New York And Ports In The Caribbean And South America.

After The Second Or Third Sunday Dinner Together, Liz Started Gently Pushing Her Little Sister To Start Dating Harold. After All, He Was Attractive To Look At. She Even Suggested That They Complete Their Relationship In Millie's Little Bedroom Down The Hall. My Mother Became Pregnant With Me Not Long After That. Even If She Hadn't Been Expecting A Kid, I Think She Would Have Married Harold Since She Saw Him As Her Best Option And Fastest Path Out Of Liz's Environment.

Whatever Part Love Played, It Was Quickly Overshadowed By The Crushing Realities Of Permanent Poverty.

One Thing Was Clear To Millie: She Didn't Want To Work For Liz And Hines's Numbers Scam. That Would Have Been Contrary To Her Core Beliefs. Consequently, She

Went Over To Park Avenue And Ninety-Seventh Street On A Daily Basis, Whether Or Not She Felt Bad In The Morning. She Was Waiting With A Ragtag Bunch Of Other Women, North Of The Border At Ninety-Sixth Street, To Be Hired As Housekeepers By The White People Who Had The Courage To Drive There.

Park Avenue Railway Lines Appeared From A Tunnel Under 97th Roadway, Transforming The Broad Roadway Of White-Gloved Doorman Buildings Into One Of Tenements With Dark Stone Arches At Each Corner. Under One Of The Arches, The Ladies Gathered. I Remember Waiting There With My Mom When I Was A Little Kid. So That She Could Keep An Eye On Me, She Always Sat Me Off To The Side, Maybe With A Few Of Other Kids. She Didn't Want Me Around In Case Potential Clients Were Passing By And Saw Us. Whenever She Was Picked, She'd Inquire With The White Lady In The Vehicle As To Whether Or Not I May Join Them. If Her New Boss Begrudgingly Allowed Me To Ride Shotgun, I'd Join Her In The Backseat. My Aunt Mabel, Who Also Frequented The Arches, Would Take Me In If The Lady Said No, Or One Of Our Many Other Acquaintances In The Area.

Millie Was Able To Do Laundry, Iron, And Sew. She Was Also Much Sought After For Saturday Night Swanky Dinner Parties Due To Her Excellent Culinary Skills. In General, The Nights Were Fruitful. But There Was This One Occasion When I Accompanied Her To Central Park West To Cook For A Wealthy Jewish Family. I Waited In The Pantry While She Cooked, Dripping With Perspiration. One Of The Dinners Got Charred. My Mother Was Smacked In The Face By The Hostess As She Rushed Through The Kitchen's Swinging Door. Thankfully, My Aunt Mabel Was There To Help Out That

Night. Mabel Flung Her Arms Around My Mother When She Saw The Wrath On Her Face And Prevented Her From Reaching For The Butcher Knife. My Mother Stormed Out Of The House, Angry And Ashamed, And I Followed, Feeling Quite Unsafe.

That Happened Thereafter. Millie Worked Till The Day Her Water Broke While She Was Carrying Me Because She Had To. It Occurred At One Of Her Day Jobs On The Upper East Side. On March 1, 1927, I Entered This World As Harold George Bellanfanti, Jr. At Lying-On Hospital On Manhattan's Jewish East Side.

South Of 96th Street On The Upper East Side, The Roaring Twenties Were Still In Full Swing, But Up In Caribbean Harlem, Where Millie And I Eventually Settled Down, The Great Depression Had Already Arrived. Or, More Precisely, They Never Departed. After I Was Born, Millie And Harold Moved Into An Apartment With Four Or Five Other Families, Generally With A Shared Bathroom Down The Hall. The Ever-Present Aromas Of Caribbean Cuisine Are Ingrained In My Earliest Recollections. Both Ours And The Ones Around Us. The Kitchen And Bathrooms Are Usually Shared, And Families Take Turns Preparing Meals. However, The Lowest Of The Impoverished Sometimes Leased Rooms Where They Had No Access To A Kitchen At All; All They Had Was A Place To Sleep.

Despite Their Grim Appearance, These Living Conditions Inspired Genuine Kindness Among The Occupants. People Shared Their Leftovers And Their Meals. "Listen, Millie, I Left Some Ackee And Saltfish, I Don't Want It To Spoil, So Use It, Darling"—Of Course, Uttered In The West Indian Lilt That Made Such Offerings All The More Endearing. Even With A Large Dripping Block Of Ice To Keep Things Cold, Food In The Iceboxes Went Rotten

Quickly. These Actions Were Motivated By More Than Just Convenience, However. Poor People Have Always Looked Out For One Another. They Live In A World Of Vulnerability, Understanding, And Compassion That The Wealthy Will Never Experience, As I Learned As A Child. I'll Never Forget The Friendships I Made While Struggling Financially, And I'll Always Consider Myself A Part Of That Community. Eventually, I Wouldn't Simply Be Saying "Hello" To The Black Waiters At Chicago's Palmer House Or To A Proud, Destitute Farmer In Senegal. It Seemed More Like A Check-In Than Anything Else.

The Sound Of My Father's Voice And The Accompanying Dread Is Another Of My First Recollections. When I Overheard Him, He Was Probably Inebriated. Since The Screaming Usually Preceded The Brutality He Inflicted On My Mother, There Was Probably Blood On His Hands And On The Bedsheets. As A Baby, All I Could Feel Was A Dark, Confining Closet Of Terror.

When I Was 18 Months Old, My Mother Brought Me On My First Trip To Jamaica. Millie's Many New York Family Members Made It Easy For Her To Leave Me In Their Care While She Went To The Office. But Harold Was Increasingly Absent As An Aboard Chef, And Millie Could No Longer Maintain Her Care For Me During The Long Hours Of The Day. My Mother And I Accompanied Harold On One Of His Reluctant Banana Boat Voyages To Jamaica, Where I Was Greeted By My Grandmother Jane With Open Arms As We Stood On The Porch Of The Modest Two-Room Cabin Where She Had Grown Up

The Children Had All Grown Up And Moved Out, And Millie's Father, The Strict One Who Had Sent Her To Work In The Fields, Had Passed Away. I'm Not Sure Whether Any Of My Earliest Recollections Of Jane Date Back To The Year We Shared An Apartment, But I Do

Recall Being Comforted By Her Voice And The Delicious Aromas Wafting From The Outside Stone Stove Where She Cooked. I Had A Little Bed With A Mattress Made Of Soft Grass And Scraps Of Old Fabric. When I First Opened My Eyes, I Saw The Exposed Wooden Rafters And Calico Curtains. All Around Me, As Far As The Eye Could See, Were Farmlands. Jane, My White Grandma, Whose Skin Was Always The Right Hue To Me, Sat On The Porch, Forever Darning Garments For One Of Her Many Grandchildren.

As I Watched Her Work One Day, I Became More Curious In The Contents Of The Sewing Basket That Was Sitting Next To Her Rocking Chair. I Reached For The Scissors And The Cloth And Got To Work. When I Reached The Fabric's Edge, I Found A Thick Border That Would Be Difficult To Cut. Angry, I Began To Yank Up At It With The Scissors. When I Finally Managed To Cut Through, A Sharp Scissor Tip Poked Me In The Right Eye.

The Sight Of Blood In My Eye Caused Me To Scream, And My Grandma Sprang To Her Feet In Shock. We Were Up In The Mountains, Far From Any Kind Of Medical Assistance, So All She Could Do Was Wipe The Eye And Put A Patch On It. All Of Jane's Tears, Worry, And Remorse Were For Nought, As Far As I Can Recall. In A Sense, I Had Made My Eyes Shut. After That, All I Could See Out Of That Eye Were Brief Flashes Of Light, Which Gradually Faded As My Ocular Muscles Wasted Away.

In Retrospect, I Attribute All Of My Early Reading Difficulties On My Impaired Eye. A Self-Inflicted Wound On My Grandmother's Porch From Long Ago Paled In Comparison To The Realization, Decades Later, That I Was Probably Dyslexic And That All My Anger And Frustration At Doing So Poorly In School And My Dropping Out Of School Halfway Through Ninth Grade

Had More To Do With That Disability Than My Grandmother's Porch.

As Soon As She Heard About The Scissors, My Mother Made Her Way To Where I Was Hiding In A Banana Boat And Snatched Me Away. She Had Relocated To A New Apartment In Harlem And Was Planning On Doing It Again. Numerous Dwellings Were Available. My Mom Left Us Often; Sometimes It Was Because She Couldn't Afford The Place, And Other Times It Was Because My Dad Was An Abusive Jerk. In Addition, Mom Would Sometimes Whisk Me Away Into The Labyrinth Of Other Immigrants' Houses When She Heard The Immigration Authorities Were On Her Trail. My Uncle Castel Had A Livery Cab And A Moving Truck, And He Drove Everyone From The Caribbean Who Was On The Run To Their Temporary Hiding Spots. The Company Did Extremely Well Financially. He And Two Other Men Would Show Up In The Dead Of Night, Pack Us Up, And Send Us On Our Way To The Next Location.

Millie's Visa Had Long Ago Expired, So The Authorities Were Hot On Her Tail. They Were Both Illegal Immigrants; She And Harold. Even Though Harold Was Also Legally Illegal, At Least He Possessed Working Documents That Allowed Him To Move Freely From Job To Job. Until My Mother Got A Divorce And Married A Citizen, Which Wouldn't Happen Until I Was Seventeen Years Old, Neither Of My Parents Could Legally Work In The United States.

This Meant That I Spent My Formative Years As A Criminal On The Run From The Law. Almost No One In The Family Would Pose For Photos, Thus We Lacked Any Documentation Of Our Time Together. When I Was Old Enough To Go Outdoors On My Own, My Mother Drilled Into Me The Importance Of Never, Ever Talking To

Strangers. She And Her Partner Used To Leave Me Alone In The Apartment On The Weekends When I Was Very Young (Perhaps About Four Years Old), But Only After I Promised Under Penalty Of Death To Never Open The Door To Anybody Who May Be There. My Mum Has Changed Her Identity And Purchased False Documents More Than Once When She Thought The Jig Could Be Up. Bellanfanti Was Shortened To Belanfonte, And Eventually Belafonte Was Derived From That. We Trembled At The Agents, But Poverty Followed Us Everywhere. My Mom Would Often Bring Me Food After Work, Claiming That She Was Fed. I Was Sure She Hadn't. Clothing Was A Luxury, As Was Everything Beyond Food, Rent, And Coal. That Terrible Winter Was The Worst. When I Started School, My Mom Had Already Accepted The Fact That She Couldn't Strike A Pact With Either God Or The Devil To Alleviate Our Family's Financial Struggles. All Mom Could Do Was Inculcate In Me And My Younger Brother, Dennis, A Set Of Core Values And Ambitions And Encourage Us To Go For The Stars. That Was The Narrative Of Every Immigrant.

But She Still Wasn't Convinced. My Mother Was Never Able To Enjoy My Success As A Singer And Actress, No Matter How Much I Achieved. She Refused To Take Any Of The Comforts I Offered Her And Instead Continued Working, Determined To Rise Above Her Status But Getting More Resentful As She Remained Where She Was.

My Mother Made Friends With A Jewish Tailor She Met On Her Way To A Park Avenue Social Club For Housewives As A Means Of Elevating Herself. She Learned To Sew And Repair Garments From The Tailor, Which Allowed Her To Supplement Her Income. And He Was A Clothier, Too. Millie Realized One Day That He

Had Left Some Of His Garments Out In The Sun For So Long That It Had Bleached The Fabric In Certain Areas. Were They, Therefore, Defective Merchandise? The Tailor Finally Conceded. But May They Be Given A Fresh Lease Of Life By Being Dyed? Of Course, The Tailor Replied, If Anybody Was Interested In Helping Out. That Was Millie. She Negotiated A Fair Price With The Tailor, Who Also Instructed Her On Which Dye Package To Use. Millie Poured A Tin Tub With Hot Water, Added The Dye, And Dipped The Clothing In It Until They Were All A Uniform Dark Blue Once Again When She Returned To Her Flat. The Procedure Was Always Fruitful. My Mother Either Sold The Clothing Or Gave Them To Me If They Didn't Sell. I Quickly Amassed A Superb Collection Of Blue Outfits For Boys. I'm Wearing A Tie I Dyed Blue, And My Mom Is Wearing Clothing She Stole From One Of Her More Kind Jobs In One Of Our Rare Family Photos. My Affinity With Jews, Which Had Begun With That Tailor But Would Grow, Is Now Much Stronger. Despite My Mother's Entrepreneurial Spirit And Her Use Of A Great Deal Of Blue Dye, She Never Managed To Lift Our Family Out Of Poverty.

After Hearing It And Other Stories About My Mother, A Doctor Eventually Requested If He Might Meet Her. I Did. After We Parted Ways, He Said That Millie Was Really Extraordinary. He Praised Her Intelligence, Noting That She Had Shown "A Genius For Survival" In The Face Of Adversity. Even Though The Hardships She Had Had Made Her Tough, She Had Never Lost Her Natural Kindness. She Used To Read Us Tales, Listen To Us, And Assist Us With Our Schoolwork When We Were Kids. She Always Reminded Us To Consider The Consequences Of Our Actions And Make Choices That Would Help Us Overcome The Obstacles We Had Faced. She Would

Always Remind Us That Escaping Poverty Wasn't The Whole Story. That Means Assisting Those In Need.

Despite Our Financial Constraints, My Mom Was Adamant About Getting Me A Beautiful Gift For My Fourth Christmas. Yes, She Bought A Used Tricycle.

I Couldn't Wait For My Dad To Take Me Out On It This Morning So I Could Ride It. Finally, About Noon, We Ventured Out Of Our Apartment And Went To The Park At 145th Street And St. Nicholas Avenue (Now The Site Of A New Apartment Complex). The Polo Grounds, Home Of The New York Giants, Could Be Seen Below Me As I Stood On That Hill. My Father Warned Me, "Never Ride Away On Your Own." Keep An Adult Close By At All Times.

The Vista Was Beautiful, And I'll Never Forget The Path That Led Down From Where We Were Standing. As I Waited For Him To Lead Me Down, My Dad Started A Conversation With Someone. He Continued Chatting Without Seeming To Realize That He Was Clutching The Tricycle's Handlebar. His Pal Was The Target Of His Double-Handed Gestures. The Trike Began Going Downward Abruptly. In My Gut, I Felt A Whoosh Of Adrenaline. Maybe I Should Have Gotten Off In The Beginning, But I Was Having Too Much Fun. The Next Thing I Knew, I Heard My Dad Shouting My Name. As I Turned Around, I Saw What Seemed To Be The Giant From "Jack And The Beanstalk" Coming Towards Me. I Cranked Up My Bike Speed To Get Away From Him. It's Too Slow. He Got Up To Me At The Foot Of The Slope And Forcibly Removed Me From The Trike. My Airborne Feet Continued To Pedal. Then He Brought Me To Some Bushes, Where He Snapped Off A Little Branch And Began Beating Me With It.

He Hit Me Again And Over Again Till I Was Soaked Through. After That, He Paused. The Sight Of Blood Seemed To Bring Him Back To Reality.

He Said Hoarsely, "You Must Never Tell Your Mother What Happened." "Let's Pretend A Group Of Kids Tried To Take Your Bike, Beat You Up, And Then I Came And Rescued You."

We Went By A Little Corner Shop On The Way Home, The Sort That Used To Sell Gum, Paper Goods, And Cigars. A White Model Yacht, With Matching White Trim, Was Displayed In The Window. That Yacht Had Always Caught My Eye. I Had Asked For It For Christmas Only A Few Weeks Previously. My Father Whispered In My Ear As We Approached That Window, "If You Don't Tell Your Mother, I'll Buy You That Boat."

My Mom Shrieked When She First Saw Me. "Oh, My God, What The Heck Happened!" She Glanced At My Dad, Wondering Whether He Had Defeated Me And Then Doubting That Anybody Could Beat Me, Even Him. He Related The Tale To Her. They Both Glanced At Me. My Feeble Nod Of Agreement Confirmed What He Had Spoken. My Mother, In A State Of Despair, Filled The Bathtub With Hot Water And Poured In A Big Amount Of Cn, A Popular Disinfectant Of The Time That Was Comparable To Iodine. She Removed My Soiled Clothing Gently, Placed Me In The Bath, And Attended To My Wounds.

As The Lash Scars Gradually Faded, She Continued This Routine For Many Days At Some Time, My Dad Went For His Next Duty Aboard Ship. I Avoided Looking At Him As He Departed Because He Gave Me A Knowing Glance. I Needed To Inform My Mom About The Situation. However, I Didn't, Not At The Time And Not Even After He Had Gone.

I Told This Experience To My Psychiatrist, Peter Neubauer, Many Years Later. When I Answered, "I Still Haven't Gotten That Boat To This Day," Peter Questioned If I Was Still Waiting For It. I Had Been Seeing Him For A While At That Point. I Reluctantly Said, "Yes," Then Calculated How Much Longer I Would Have To Lie On His Sofa.

After The Event, I Frequently Pondered Why My Father Chose To Frighten Me In Such A Manner. In Fact, It Happened Several Times. One Thing Was Certain; He Had A Vicious Side. And Yet, I Know That My Mom Had A Hand In Its Release. My Parents' Marriage Was Terrible And Full Of Misunderstandings. My Dad Used To Grope My Mom In Those Cramped Quarters In A Sexually Suggestive Way, Particularly After He'd Been Away And They'd Both Had A Few Drinks. Even Though She Slapped His Hand, I Could See That She Enjoyed His Contact. I Remember Hearing Groans Whenever Either Of My Parents Closed The Door To Their Bedroom Or Drew A Makeshift Curtain Across The Opening. I Saw Firsthand How Sex Might Transform Its Participants Into New Persons. However, Not Entirely, And Not For Very Long. One Of The Things I Learnt About Sex, If Unconsciously, Was That When Alcohol Was Involved, It Was No Longer A Means By Which Two People Could Express Their Genuine Emotions To One Another, But Rather An Exercise In Unreality That Might Be Rather Frightening: A Bacchanal. My Mother's Tirades Against My Father, For His Drinking And Philandering, His Being An Absent Husband And Father, And His Failing To Provide Adequately, Would Resume As Soon As The Effects Of The Alcohol Wore Off. Because Of Her Father's Infidelity And The Terrible Way He Crushed Her Hopes And Goals, I Believe She Learnt Early On Not To Put Much Faith In

Males. She Was Particularly Vicious When She Began Attacking My Dad. I Believe She Castrated Him By Making Him Question His Masculinity, And That As A Result, Dad Took His Anger Out On Me, His Failed Attempt At Being A Parent And A Man.

I Was Four And A Half When My Mother Brought My Infant Brother, Dennis, Home, And Even I Could See That My Father's Temper Had Worsened. Dennis Was Much Fairer Than The Rest Of Us; He Also Had Extremely Sandy Hair And Gray Eyes, None Of Which I Noticed Until I Was A Little Older. It Seems That My Father Did Not Approve. That Perplexed Me, Since I Knew That The Lighter Someone's Complexion, The Better In The Eyes Of My Parents And Their Friends. Blue Eyes Were Considered Superior To Brown Or Black Ones, While Wavy Hair Was Seen As More Desirable Than Kinky Hair In The West Indian Caste System. However, The Contrasts With Dennis Were Too Stark To Ignore. My Mother Told Me The News That My Father No Longer Considered The Baby To Be His Later In Life. That Pushed My Mom To An Extreme Of Rage And Hurt From Which She Never Fully Recovered. My Dad Should Have Understood That Characteristics Passed Down From One Generation Sometimes Reappear In Mixed Households Two Or Three Generations Later. Polygamy Among Parents Or Grandparents Further Confused The Genetic Mix On The Islands. It's Possible That A Kid Of A Lesbian Couple Might Inherit The Light Blue Eyes Of The Father. You May Lose Your Spouse And Your Relationship If You Accused Them Of Wrongdoing And Then Publicly Called Them Out On It. My Mom Tried To Get My Dad To See Reason, But He Was Unmovable. Their Marriage, Such As It Was, Hung By A Thread.

My Mother Used To Leave Dennis In My Care When She Went To Work During The Day Or On The Weekend. After All, She Had No One Else To Turn To For Support. But What Should She Do? That's How I Felt About It, At Least, Until My Psychiatrist Raised A Hand Years Later. Let's Take A Step Back, He Suggested. "You Were Accountable For Your Sibling."

There Was A Nod From Me.

In Other Words, "You Were Always Told You Should Take Care Of Him, Look Out For Him, Babysit, And Make Him Dinner Sometimes."

That's Correct, I Agreed With Her.

The Doctor Inquired Softly, "How Old Were You?"

As The Truth Dawned On Me, I Felt Like I Needed To Take A Deep Breath. "Maybe Five Or Six," I Finally Volunteered. Something Clicked At That Point, And The Floodgates Of Tears Opened. Anger, Disillusionment, And Fury Cried Out In Tears. I Felt Anger At My Mom, Whom I Had Always Defended. I Was Also Furious With My Brother For Forcing Me Into This Intimidating Position. I Was Only Five Years Old When I Learned That My Mother Was Out In The World Performing That Soul-Crushing Labor, And That With My Father Gone So Much, It Was Up To Me To Assist Her Find A Way Out Of, Or At Least To Cope With, Her Abject Poverty. I Didn't Feel Like I Could Blame My Mom For My Current Predicament Or Whine About The Weight Of Adulthood That Had Been Thrust Upon Me. I Needed To Show Her, And Myself, That I Wouldn't Leave Her As My Dad Did. My Deepest Fear Was That Mom Would Tell Me, "You're Just Like Your Father." I Always Collapsed Whenever She Did It.

It Was As If A Drawer I'd Kept Locked For Decades Had Finally Opened, And I Could Feel All The Terror And Pain Of A Five-Year-Old Child.

A Long-Forgotten Recollection Was Stored In That Drawer, Much Like A Faded Black-And-White Photograph. It Was A Saturday During The Winter, And It Was Already Late In The Day; The Sky Was Already Becoming Black. While My Mom Was At Work, I Had Cared For Dennis All Day. In Addition To Being Hungry And Exhausted, All I Wanted Was My Mother's Approval For Being Such A Responsible And Mature Elder Son. Instead, She Silently Made Her Way Across The Room To Our Bed In Our Studio Apartment. She Stared Into The Void With A Profound Sense Of Sorrow. After Some Time, I Finally Asked Her What Was Wrong. As She Removed Her Hat, Fighting Back Tears That Would Not Be Denied, She Said, "When You Grow Up, Son, Never Ever Go To Bed At Night Knowing That There Was Something You Could Have Done During The Day To Strike A Blow Against Injustice And You Didn't Do It." She Retreated Into Quiet, Allowing Me To Ponder The Significance Of Her Terse Instruction.

It Was The One Moment In My Life That Would Always Stand Out As The Rosebud.

My Mother's Shift Toward Religion As Their Separation Progressed Had Significant Effects On Me.

Millie Was Raised In The Hills Of St. Ann Parish, So She Was No Stranger To The Evangelists Who Held Forth From Makeshift Shacks. They Hadn't Even Tried To Help Her. My Mom Often Said That Holy Roller Was "Too Niggerish," Which Meant That It Was Too Religious. However, Catholicism Was A Whole Other Animal. My Mother Was Enamored By Its Air Of Mystery And Grandeur. She Favored The Holy Ghost Out Of The

Father, Son, And Holy Spirit. She Became Further Ensconced In The Church, Her Need On Jesus Becoming Stronger By The Day As Her Immigration Ambitions Faded And Her Marriage Crumbled. The Weight Of My Mother's Faith Ultimately Fell On My Father. He Became Even More Devout A Catholic Than The Pope In An Effort To Prove His Love For Her. When I Became Too Large For Him To Beat Up On, I'd Sometimes Spout Forth Some Blasphemies That Really Shook Him To His Core. In An Effort To Protect Himself From A Potential Curse, He Would Frantically Make Three Or Four Signs Of The Cross With His Fingers. If These Plays Were Performed Outside, He Would Back Away From Me So That The Bolt Of Lightning Representing God's Vengeance Wouldn't Miss Its Mark.

Personally, I Didn't Had A Say In The Situation. Every Week, Dressed In One Of My Little Blue Outfits, I Accompanied My Mother To Catholic Worship. St. Charles Borromeo, On West 142nd Street Between Seventh And Eighth Avenues, Was The Name Of The Catholic School I Attended. When I Did Badly On Reading Tests, The Nuns Would Beat My Knuckles With Great Force. I Kept Searching Their Expressions For Remorse, But There Was None To Be Seen. They Didn't Appear To Like Either The Instruction Or The Learning Process. I Could See That Working In This Grim Corner Of Harlem Was Nothing More Than A Test For Them. Knowing That Nothing But The Bleak Triumph Of Spending Time In Penance Awaited Me At That School, I Dragged Myself There Every Day With A Heavy Heart.

Now That My Dad Is Gone For Long Stretches Of Time, I've Turned To Uncle Lenny, One Of My Mom's Numerous Brothers, To Act As A Surrogate Father. Like Hines, Uncle Lenny Was A Financial Tycoon Who Ran His

Own Bank. He Was A Large, Ruggedly Attractive Guy With A Barrel Chest. My Mother Was The Only One Who Ever Dared To Cross Uncle Lenny. When He Entered A Pub, A Group Of Admirers And Subordinates Would Immediately Form A Circle Around Him. My Mother Once Dispatched Me To The Local Tavern In An Attempt To Locate Him. While I Was Talking To Him, A Large Black Police Officer Walked In, Fully Uniformed. As They Continued To Argue, Lenny Abruptly Turned Around And Cold-Cocked Him. Just One Jab! I've Seen Yam Bags Being Unloaded From Ships. This Officer Fell More Heavily Than That. Upon Seeing Him, Lenny Smiled Down At Me, Said, "Come On, Boy," Walked Over Him, And We Were On Our Way. Incredibly, Nothing Happened Since The Police Officer Was Presumably Disputing His Compensation.

It Was Always Exciting To Run Into Lenny On The Street And Hear Him Say, "Harry, Come With Me." It Meant I Could Go Along On His Numbers Rounds And Sometimes Get A Lollipop Or Even A Cent For My Trouble. We Frequented Cuban Cigar Shops, Which Often Concealed Underground Gambling Activities Behind Their Humidors. However, When Shopping For Yams, Pawpaws, And Gingerroot, You Might Also Play The Numbers. Lenny's Runners Took Care Of Collecting The Money And Taking Bets, While Lenny Himself Enjoyed Making Social Calls To The Shop Owners. "It's Good For Business," Harry Said. There, Among The Lovely Aromas Of Aftershave And Cheap Perfume, We Would Often Find Ourselves Chatting With The Local Males. Sucking On A Lollipop, I Would Settle Into One Of The Red Leather Seats Along The Wall And Listen To The Recap Of Yesterday Night's Boxing Battle At Madison Square

Garden. It Was Another Victory For Joe Louis. Is There Anybody A Black Guy Couldn't Win A Fight Against? Though She Avoided Meddling As Much As Possible, My Mother Would Sometimes Bring Lenny A Box With The Day's Wagers From Her Building Or Block. Because Lenny Provided Us Money To Carry Us Through The Week Practically Every Sunday, She Had Little Room To Reject. Back In The 1930s, It Could Get You A Lot Of Food. We All Knew Lenny Was Inebriated When He Walked In Looking So Stern. He Often Told His Son, "You Know How Lucky You Are, Boy, That You Got Your Mother?" "Obey Her From Now On, Or Else!" Lenny Would Then Begin To Weep. You Should Adore Your Mother; I Abandoned Mine In The Islands A Long Time Ago. Lloyd, Lenny's Kid, Was Still Living With His Mother, From Whom He Had Become Alienated. Lenny Carried A Long, White Silk Handkerchief In His Back Pocket, Which He Often Removed To Snap And Use As A Tissue After A Runny Nose. My Mom Threatened To Come Over And Grab Him By The Tie If He Didn't Stop. "Pull It Together, Dude!" This Would Be A Shock To Lenny. Only She Could Have Communicated With Him In Such A Manner.

Our Family Godfather Lenny Was The One Who Warned Me Against Holding Him Up As An Example. Inebriatedly, He Would Sob, "I Don't Want Any Of You To Grow Up Like Me," And Pull Out The Handkerchief Once Again. Most Of The Prominent African-Americans Of The Day Called Harlem Home And Mixed Freely With The Locals There, Unlike In The Posh Neighborhoods South Of 96th Street Where They Were Barred From Entry. Duke Ellington Would Be Out Doing Some Grocery Shopping While Wearing A Do-Rag, While Langston Hughes Would Be At The Neighborhood Watering Hole. Brotherhood Of Sleeping Car Porters Leader A. Philip Randolph Was One

Of My Idols. Randolph Started The Union And Eventually Defeated The Pullman Company In A Bloody Campaign For Higher Wages And Less Work Hours For His 7,000 Members. While I Was Unaware Of The Specifics, My Mother Assured Me That Randolph Had Successfully Led A Strike. In Other Words, He Was A Heroic Figure. I Enjoyed Seeing Him March Through Harlem With His Men In Full Regalia, Complete With Red Hats Cocked Just So And Gleaming Red Collars. The Porters Were Held In High Esteem Not Just Because Of The Generous Pay That Randolph Had Secured For Them, But Also Because Of Their Broad Travels And Advanced Educations. They Were The Working Class' Equivalent Of The Professional Elite (Doctors And Attorneys). If Someone Had Told Me When I Was Six Or Seven That I Would Be A Sleeping-Car Porter, I Would Have Been Ecstatic. Instead, I Would Have Been Very Perplexed To Discover That I Would Meet Randolph At The Height Of The Civil Rights Movement Thanks To Martin Luther King, Jr.

When The Campaign Finally Took Off, It Was Already Too Late For Hollywood To Change Its Portrayal Of The Proud Train Porters As Happy, Subservient "Darkies." The Genuine Ones, Who Were Savvy And Confident, Had Had Lengthy Discussions With Their Passengers Of All Races Late Into The Night. They Carried Bags And Caught Gratuities With A Pleased "Thank You, Suh!" From The White Leading Men And Women Whose Storylines They Floated In And Out Of In Hollywood.

Particularly Damaging To The Reputation Of These Once Proud Servicemen Was A Brief Mack Sennett Silent Picture. A Wealthy White Adulterer And His Weekly Mistress Board A Luxurious Pullman Train. The Cheater's Wife Boards The Train, But She Doesn't Know It. From Now On, The Adulterer, His Wife, And His Mistress Will

Engage In A Series Of Comedic Routines In Which They Will Enter And Exit Their Respective Staterooms With Just The Narrowest Of Escapes, Forcing The Adulterer To Narrowly Avert Many Heart Attacks. A Black Uncle Tom Porter With Bug-Eyed Humility Is The Only Other Person Who Knows The Truth Except The Adulterous. The Wealthy White Adulterer Rewards The Faithful Porter With A Gratuity Every Time They Pass One Other In This Comical Routine For Keeping His Mouth Shut. Every Time This Occurs, The Porter Will Bow, Smile, And Bite The Coin To Ensure It Is Genuine. And So It Goes, As Always. At The Conclusion Of The Journey, Neither Woman Is Any The Wiser, And The Adulterer, Who Has Been Saved From A Dreadful End, Tips And Winks His Appreciation At The Porter. This Pretty Stupid Piece, From The Early Days Of Hollywood, Altered The Public's Perception Of Porters In A Fundamental Way. A Devastating Blow To An Inspiring Bunch Of Black Guys!

West Indians, Like Myself, Looked Up To Achievers Of Any Race, Therefore I Had White Role Models As Well. My Mom Looked Forward To Every Fireside Talk Given By President Roosevelt; She Looked Forward To Both Roosevelt And Eleanor. I, Too, Had Great Respect For Them, But I Had No Idea That A Phone Call From Mrs. Roosevelt Would Lead To A Relationship That Would Alter The Course Of My Life. Almost Every Performer I Watched On Film Was Fantastic, But My Favorites Were The Tough Guys Like Jimmy Cagney, George Raft, And Edward G. Robinson. The Police, The Fbi, The Banks With Their Condescending White Tellers Who'd Never Given Us A Break—These Were The Enemies They Fought On Our Behalf, And They Were Our Folk Heroes, Our Working-Class Heroes. We'd Be Rooting For Them To Put Guns To The Tellers' Heads. They Acted As Our Masked

Saviors. Get Out Of Here With That Cash! In Addition To White Actors, I Also Looked Up To White Athletes Like The Ferocious Boxer Jimmy Braddock. The Great Black Deity Who Would Soon Knock Braddock Out, Joe Louis, Overshadowed All Of This For A Young Child In The 1930s.

Louis Resided In Detroit, But He Spent A Lot Of Time In Harlem Because He Trained In A Camp In Lakewood, New Jersey, For His Bouts In New York. Someone On The Street Might Remark, "Hey, I Heard Joe Louis Is Over On One Hundred And Twenty-Fifth And Lenox." Let's Go Check To See If He's Still Around. We'd Rush There, Find Out That He Was Eating Lunch At A Nearby Establishment, And Then Strain Our Faces Against The Glass To Get A Sight Of The Living Legend.

Lenny Had Already Assured Me That We Would Go To Lakewood To See The Great Champ Practice. But He Had To Hold Out Until The Once-Or-Twice-Yearly Bouts Louis Had Booked At Madison Square Garden. Louis Covered The Expenses Of The Camp By Allowing People To Travel Over On Sundays For A Few Weeks Before To These Great Events And Purchase Tickets. Lenny Stopped By In His Shiny Black Packard One Sunday While My Dad Was Home From Work To Drive Us To Lakewood, Where Louis Was Back In Training Across The River. Even Though I Was Dressed And Ready To Leave, My Mother Became Angry With Me For Whatever Reason I Cannot Remember. My Punishment Was To Remain At Home By Myself Instead Of Going With The Rest Of The Team To Training Camp. My Mom Was Adamant, But My Dad Attempted To Argue My Point. And Then, To To My Surprise, He Answered, "Well, Then I'll Stay, Too." After Millie And Lenny Left, Dad Brought Me Up To The Top Of The Building To Play Marbles In His Street Clothes.

Even Now, Over 75 Years Later, When I Think Back On His Compassion—A Rare Gesture, But No Less True Because Of Its Rarity—I Have To Pause And Blink Back Tears. I Don't Know Whether It Was The Same Guy Who Brutally Beat Me Or The One Who Played Marbles With Me On The Roof That Day. Perhaps Both Of These Things Are True. But I Still Don't Know For Sure.

My Whole Roster Of Heroes Expanded When We Finally Upgraded To An Arc-Shaped Rca Radio. The Green Hornet, The Lone Ranger, And Amos And Andy, Two White Comic Book Characters That Sounded Just As Black To Us As They Did To The Rest Of America, Are Just A Few Examples. The Radio Was Also The Medium Via Which I Discovered That I Could Really Had Musical Talent. My Mom And I Used To Sing Together In The Kitchen Whenever One Of Our Favorite Songs Came On The Radio. As A Result, My Mom Encouraged Me To Perform In Front Of Our Extended Family. Everything Here Is Quite Tame. There's An Ancient Irish Song About Moms That Goes Something Like This: "M Is For The Million Things She Gave Me, / O Means Only That She's Growing Old, / T Is For The Tears She Shed To Save Me, / H Is For The Heart As Pure As Gold..." An Additional Setting Of "I Think That I Shall Never See / A Poem Lovely As A Tree." I Didn't Give My Voice Nearly Enough Credit, But I Now Realize That I Learned A Lot About How To Use It By Performing These Parlor Tricks.

A Little Distance Away, At The Apollo Theatre, Was More Music, And Much Better Music. As A Small Boy Of Seven, I Used To Adore Dressing Up In My Nicest Blue Suit And Heading To The Apollo After Sunday Mass To See Cab Calloway, Count Basie, Duke Ellington, Lucky Millinder, Billie Holiday, Or Ella Fitzgerald Perform. Even Though The Service Seemed To Last Forever, I Was Able To Get

Through It Because I Knew That In Just A Few Short Hours I Would Be In The True Spiritual Cathedral. All Of Them Performed At The Apollo, And My Mom Found A Way To Take Me There. Or, If She Had To Work, To Send My Dad Or Another Relative With Me.

When I Got Home From School One Day, I Saw Two Guys Trudging Up The Four Floors To Our Apartment With A Rented Stand-Up Roller Piano, So I Guess She Must Have Begun Harboring Hopes That I May Join That Eternal Pantheon. You May Play It Like A Regular Piano Or Insert Paper Rolls And Let It Play On Its Own. My Mother Told Me I Would Have To Take Courses From Miss Shepherd At A Cost Of Fifty Cents Each Session If I Wanted To Learn.

Miss Shepherd Was A Single Mother Who Taught Piano And Violin Lessons While Wearing A Long Dress, A High-Collared Shirt, And Pince-Nez Spectacles. Nearby Neighborhoods Regarded Her As The Most Talented Music Educator. Equally Stringent. When I Messed Up When Playing Scales, She Would Smack My Fingers With A Ruler Just As Hard As The Nuns. In Other Words, It Hurt Like Hell. Eventually, I Began Skipping Her Courses In Favor Of Spending Time On The Streets, Where I Would Often Engage In Marbles For Purees Games With Some Of The Rougher Kids In My Area. I Was Terrified When My Mom Walked By And Saw Me. Her Expression Became Grim As She Dragged Me Off To Miss Shepherd's House. There Was No Hiding The Fact That I Had Missed Weeks Of School. "Harry, Do You Have Any Idea What I Had To Do To Pay For All Those Fifty Cent Lessons?"

My Failure To Live Up To Her Expectations Was The First (But Certainly Not The Last) Blow To Her Immigrant Ideal Of Giving Up All For The Sake Of Her Children.

My Mom Finally Got Rid Of The Piano That Week. When Mom Finally Told Me, "You're On Your Own Now," I Felt A Sense Of Relief. Of Course, I Did.

Chapter 3

Despite My Family's Best Efforts, I Had Developed Into A Challenging Kid By The Time I Was Seven. At Home And On The Way To School, When I Was Often Confronted By Young Irish And Italians Who Saw No Reason Not To Start A Fight With A Black Boy On His Own, I Gave As Good As I Got. Most Of The Children At Their P.S. 186 On 145th Street, A Five-Story Redbrick Building Between Broadway And Amsterdam Avenue, Were White, Which Only Served To Incite Greater Conflict. I Wandered The Corridors Like A Time Bomb, Waiting For The Moment When Some Careless Kid Bumps Into Me. This Was A Common Occurrence.

My Mother's Responses To These Fights Were Intense And At Times Confusing. She Once Provided Me With A Secondhand White Blouse I Needed For A School Play While I Was In Elementary School. That Clothing Meant A Lot To Me Since I Knew How Much My Mother Had Sacrificed To Provide For Me. I Saw Her Fix It And Stitch On A Missing Button While Listening To Amos 'N' Andy The Night Before The Show. The Following Day, I Felt Great, And The Performance Went Off Without A Hitch. But While I Was Walking Home That Day, A Gang Of Lads Attacked Me And Viciously Teased Me. Despite My Anger, I Chose To Ignore Them So That My New Clothing Wouldn't Be Ruined. They Got The Courage To Start Pushing Me About And Eventually Hitting Me. I Set Off Running And Got Away From Them After A Few Blocks. It Was Pure Chance That I Encountered My Mom In The Driveway Of Our Home. She Insisted On Being Told The Whole Story. I Could See The Rage Building In Her Eyes As I Told Her This. To Find My Aggressors, She Led Me Back To The Spot. We Eventually Located Them, And At

That Point She Snatched My Books And Jacket And Told Me To "Go Do What You Got To Do!" My Mind Was Boggled. She Steered Me Toward The Group's Greatest Bully. She Shouted, "Get Him!" In A Hoarse Voice. I Was So Elated By Her Support That I Stomped The Man. I Was More Than Just A Little Bloodied When I Finally Made It Through. It Shocked Me When Everyone Else Suddenly Began Running Away. When I Looked Around, My Mom Was Beaming At Me. As My Eyes Welled With Tears, I Wrapped My Arms Around Her Waist In The Most Bearlike Embrace I Could Muster. I Told My Mother, "Thank You So Much For Your Assistance." She Gave Me A Return Embrace. There's More To Life Than Meeting Your Basic Needs," She Informed Me.

When I Got Home From School, I Wandered Aimlessly, Maybe Too Aimlessly. I Was Playing On The Street And Was Struck By A Vehicle Once. When I Awoke At Harlem Hospital, I Saw That My Leg Was Fractured And Dangling In Traction From A Cast That Reached To My Waist. As Usual, My Mom Put The Blame On My Dad. A Guy Of Honor Who Can Keep The Family Together Would Be Ideal. When I Cut My Eye With The Scissors, Mom Blamed Me, But She Also Held Some Of The Responsibility.

The Hospital Medications I Was Given Caused Severe Chapping Of My Lips And Constant Thirst. I Discovered That A Certain Method Of Sucking Stimulated My Salivary Glands Into Action. By The Time I Got Home, I Was So Used To It That A Sizable Lump Had Formed Under One Of My Bottom Lips. Now, Though, I Just Had To Keep Sucking. My Mom Gave It Her All. She Taped Up The Bump, And I Removed It. She Covered It With Bitters Or Spicy Sauce, And I Sucked On It Until The Unpleasant

Flavor Disappeared. In The End, She Enlisted My Dad's Help.

"Boy, If You Suck That Lip Again, You'll Regret It," My Father Cautioned Me. But I Managed To Pull It Off. The Penalty Matched The Severity Of The Offence. My Father Shoved Me Into The Bed And Wedged His Powerful Legs Around Me. Then He Put One Hand Under My Chin And Held Me There. He Extended His Cigar With His Free Hand And Blew The Ash Away. Its Glowing Crimson Flame Was A Sight To See. The Question: "You Want To Suck Your Lip?" The Ember Grew In Proximity To The Bump On My Lip. What Do You Mean, "You Want To Suck It?" The Ember Inched Closer Once Again, This Time By Two. I Could Feel The Heat Coming Off Of It, And Just In Time He Took It Away Before It Could Burn Me. He Took His Belt And Began To Whip Me.

My Mother Argued That It Would Be Safer To Return Me To Jamaica, Where I Was Born, Since There I Was Less Likely To Be Struck By A Vehicle. I Traveled Down With My Dad On A United Fruit Company Boat While Dennis Remained In Harlem With My Mom. I Spent My Time While Not In His Quarters Seeing Him Prepare And Serve The Three Daily Meals For The Ship's Officers And Staff. The Vacation Revealed A Different Side Of Him To Me. He Was In Charge Of All The Kitchen Staff And Gave Orders With Impressive Speed. Despite My Reservations And Animosity, I Found Myself Admiring Him.

Aboukir Was The Name Of The Mountain Community Where My Grandma Jane Formerly Resided. Her Home Was A Wooden Structure Set Into The Hillside On Stilts, With A Roof Made From Scraps Of Zinc And Wood From Neighboring Ocho Rios. There Was No Power, So As Night Fell, Jane Turned On The Oil Lamps. There Was Also No Indoor Plumbing, Just An Outhouse In The

Backyard. Jane Cultivated Plantains, Yams, Passion Fruit, Okra, Callaloo, And The Indigenous Fruit Ackee, Which You Cooked (And Boiled) On Her Little Piece Of Land. Her Extended Family And Adult Children Shared Her Lifestyle. On The Once-Vast Plantations That Had Been Divided Up, Everyone Got Their Own Little Home And An Acre Or Two Of Land. The Islanders Had Vivid Memories Of Life Before They Had Their Own Land, Since Colonial Rule Was Only Just Beginning To Fade. Like Lord Mountbatten Looking Out Over His Expansive Estate, They Cared Deeply For Those Parcels Of Land.

The Affection And Comfort I Received From My Grandma When I Was A Baby Was Intensified When I Was An Adult. She Loved Me, And I Adored Her Right Back. Jane Love Was The Matriarch Of A Huge Family, And She Continued To Fix The Clothing Of Her Children, Grandkids, And Other Relatives, But I Always Felt Like She Made An Exception For Me. Maybe It Was Because I Was The One Coming From A Long Distance. Maybe She Sensed My Distress And Treated Me With Extra Tenderness And Care. Perhaps Feeling Responsible For The Scissors Incident Made Her More Caring. There Has Never Been A More Fitting And Deserving Last Name Than Hers, As Far As I'm Concerned.

The Two Of Us Together Had A Significant And Unique Impact On My Life. For The Rest Of My Life, I Would Have An Unusual Comfort Level Interacting With People Of Different Races And Socioeconomic Backgrounds. This Would Serve Me Well In My Careers As An Entertainer And, Later, As An Activist, When I Was Asked To Mediate Between Martin Luther King And His Southern Baptist Followers On The One Hand And The Irish, Patrician Kennedy Clan On The Other. That's Because Jane, Who Was As Pure White And Blue-Eyed As A Human Can Be,

Showered Me With So Much Affection. "I Need To Find Harry." I Still Remember What She Said. "Where Are You, My Darling Harry?"

Many Of Her Followers Frequented Her House For Meals On A Daily Basis, Not Only Because They Shared Her Passion For Jane But Also Because She Prepared Delicious Meals. She Could Only Rely On Her Outside, Stone-Hewn Wood Stove. Not All Of The Fruits And Vegetables She Grew Were Available Year-Round, So She Didn't Have Much Of A Crop To Work With. She Ate Mostly Chicken For Protein. But She Enjoyed It All Year Long. Jane Hatched Forth As Many Chicks As She Could Handle, And Then Some. If We Could Have Helped Her Spawn Any More, She Would Have Had Us Sleep On Eggs. Even Though Chicken Was On The Menu Almost Every Night, Jane Always Managed To Make It Taste Different By Adding New Spices, Switching Up The Other Ingredients, And Cooking The Chicken In Different Ways. Sated And Content, Her Visitors Eventually Made Their Way Home Down The Shadowy Roads, Each Turning On Their Own Oil Light In The Nearby Hills As They Disappeared.

I Had To Make My Way Alone To A One-Room Schoolhouse Every Morning, Where I Spent Hours Each Day Trying To Learn To Read While Feeling Nothing But Anger And Frustration. Jane May Have Me Do An Errand In The Next Village After That. There Were Gigantic Concrete Tanks, Open-Topped, Some Aboveground And Others Belowground, That I Would Pass On The Mountainous Trails Leading From One Community To Another. Our Sole Supply Of Potable Water Was The Rainwater Stored In These Containers. Water Was Sluiced Into Our Bottles And Barrels Through Zinc Funnels That Protruded From The Tanks; I Avoided Them

Like The Plague Since They Seemed Like Enormous Arms Reaching Out To Grab Me. My Worries Were Reasonable. People Sometimes Fell In, And If The Tank's Water Level Was Too Low, They Were Trapped. They Risked Drowning If Nobody Found Them, And Sometimes They Did.

The Locals Would Load Up Their Donkeys And Carts With Their Produce And Go To Brown's Town, The Closest Market, To Sell It. When Their Carts Were Overflowing, The Women Would Cover Their Heads In Bright Bandannas And Continue Transporting Goods. Sometimes I'd Get To Go Along With An Uncle, Either Walking Behind Or, More Excitingly, Riding Shotgun On The Donkey. Sometimes I Was Able To Grab A Ride On One Of The Few Vehicles In The Area, Shouting, "Don't Crush The Banana!" "Hey, Mon, You Want A Fender Ride?" I'd Ask, Then Climb Up On The Fender And Grab On To The Window Frame As We Rolled Along The Dirt Roads, Eventually Passing A Group Of Bauxite Workers On Their Way Home, Their Cheeks Red From The Dust.

Ocho Rios, With Its Deepwater Dock, Was The Primary Destination For United Fruit Company Banana Exports. The Ufc Tallyman Counted And Paid For The Shipment Of Bananas, Sugarcane, Mangoes, And Oranges. Not By Accident Did The Song That Became My Hallmark Include The Lyrics, "Come, Mr. Tally Man, Tally Me Banana, / Daylight Come And Me Wan' Go Home."

I Would Accompany The Guys As They Shopped For The Enamel Pots And Store-Bought Rockers That Their Wives Had Requested After They Were Paid. Their Trucks Would Rattle Along The Roads As Their Headlights Scoured The Fields, And They Would Even Stop At The Local Bar For A Few Shots Before Heading Home. I

Feigned To Be Clinging On For Dear Life While Perched On The Fender In The Chill Of The Night.

My Father Brought Me On One Of His Banana Boat Voyages Back To New York After School Was Out. Now That I Was Eight Years Old, I Could Get Into Much More Serious Mischief.

During That Summer, I Became Friends With A Girl Called Eleanor In Our New Multi-Family Apartment Because We Both Enjoyed Pretending To Be Doctors. I Can Still See The Scenario In My Head As Clearly As I Did At The Time. The Kitchen Is Off To The Left. Bedroom, This Way Please. The Canning Pantry Takes Center Stage As A Linking Element Between The Several Rooms. In The Bedroom, A Young Boy And Girl Are Fumbling With One Other's Buttons. In The Kitchen, The Boy's Mom Is Busy Preparing Dinner. The Heavy Curtain That Separates The Bedroom From The Pantry Is Usually Drawn. To Communicate With Her Kid, Who May Be In His Bedroom, Without Leaving The Kitchen Today, The Mother Slips Aside The Curtain. There Is A Complete Standstill Among The Kids. The Young Woman Runs Offstage. Both Mom And Son Gaze At Each Other In Shock. At Long Last, Mom Gets A Word In. This One's For Your Dad, I Promise.

My Dad, Who Was Typically Out Of Town, Was Oddly Present That Week. After Two Days Of Silence, I Dared Hope That I Would Be Able To Avoid This New And Dreadful Type Of Punishment. Then, One Sunday As I Was Getting Ready To Go To Church, My Dad Grabbed Me And Dragged Me Into The Restroom. I Checked Out The Tub And Found That It Was Full Of Boiling Water. You Realize Why We're Doing This, Right?"

I Chose Not To Respond.

"Dress In Nothing But A Towel."

With Great Deliberation, I Began To Disrobe. To Think He Was Going To Force Me Into That Tub Was Unbelievable To Me. When I Began To Weep, He Smacked Me In The Face. I Changed Out Of My Clothes And Stopped Weeping. I Had Accepted My Absolute Horror. I Was Prepared To Take Charge. Maybe I Just Mentally Checked Out For A While.

My Dad Grabbed Me Just As I Was About To Walk Into The Water. My Mother Had To Stop Him From Severely Belting Me For The Second Time. I Found Myself Blaming Both Him And Her. The Nature Of Her Punishment Was A Mystery To Her. But She Had To Realize It Would Go To Such Lengths.

My Aunt Liz And Uncle Lenny Were The Ones Who First Sparked My Interest In Mathematics. Almost Everyone In My Environment, Even The Impoverished And The Desperate, Seemed Excited By The Prospect Of Playing The Numbers. Money Could Do So Much: Cover Rent, Mend Relationships, And Provide Temporary Satisfaction. That's Why I Shouldn't Have Been Surprised When I Found Myself Playing Three-Card Monte On The Street One Day. My Mom Could Use The Ten Bucks My Aunt Liz Gave Me To Buy Some Necessities. After Seeing The Three-Card Monte Dealer, All I Could Think About Was The Possibility Of Increasing That Bill By Taking A Risk. So I Did, And The Ten Bucks Vanished Overnight.

Concerned That I May Not Have Enough Cash On Me, I Hurried Back To My Aunt's Flat. Runners Were Preparing To Deliver Bundles Of Cash That Had Been Spread Out On The Mattresses Of The Bedrooms Down The Corridor. I Quietly Entered A Bedroom And Removed A 10 Dollar Cash From One Of The Envelopes. I Really Doubt That Aunt Liz Would Miss The Cash Or Even Suspect That I Stole It. But She Managed To Pull It Off.

Business Eagle That She Was, She Saw The Shortage That Same Day, Ruled Out Everyone Except Me As The Likely Perpetrator. We Didn't Have A Phone, So She Couldn't Contact My Mom, But She Informed Her When They Next Saw Each Other. My Mom's Response Was One Of Moral Outrage. To Accuse My Kid In Such A Way!" She Shot Back Angrily. I Listened In The Background, Sick With Guilt And Unable To Say What I Had Done, Until The Conversation Heated Up To The Point Where My Mother Ordered Her Sister What To Do With Herself. And I, Red With Embarrassment, Had To Spend The Remainder Of Aunt Liz's Life Pretending She Hadn't Wronged Me.

That Day, I Realized I Shouldn't Take Money From My Gaming Account, But I Didn't Stop Playing Altogether. When I Was A Kid, My Friends And I Used Cigar Boxes To Play A Game Where We Had To Win Marbles. The "Dealer" Would Make Three Little Roman Arches On One Side Of The Box And Place It In The Street Gutter Downhill. The Goal Of The Game Was To Have Your Marble Land In One Of The Holes From A Distance Of Five To 10 Feet. If It Landed In The Single Opening, The Other Miniature Gamblers Owed You One Purée Marble In Exchange For Your Successful Attempt. The Two-Puree Hole Is Better, And The Three-Puree Hole Is Best Of All. Your Stone Was Lost If It Didn't Fit Through Any Of The Openings.

From The Time I Was A Kid Playing For Purees On The Street To The Time I Was A Teen In The Military To The Time I Returned To Harlem And Played Poker For Sometimes Fairly Significant Sums, I Never Went Over My Limit. When I Finally Made It To Sin City, I Was Finally Going To Give In To The Temptation Of Gambling

Beyond My Means And Keep Playing Until I Had To Stop—For Good.

My Mom Thought It Was Time To Get Us Kids Out Of Harlem And Back To Jamaica For A While, Where We Could Be Safe And Away From The City's Many Temptations. My Brother Dennis And I Would Go To A Real British School, And My Mom Would Finally Have A Job. She Assured Us She Would Remain And Even Brought Her Own Suitcase. It Was 1936; Dennis Was Five; I Was Nine. Nothing Went According To Plan For Any Of Us.

For Two Or Three Weeks, My Mother Looked For Employment While We Slept In A Little Leased One-Room Home Near One Of My Aunts In Kingston. Sadly, There Was None. One Day I Came Upon Her Loading Her Belongings Back Into Her Trunk; She Was Somber And Dejected, Her Lips Set In A Line. I Did Not Inquire As To Her Actions Or Motivations. I Knew.

My Mother Enrolled Me In The Boarding Program At Morris-Knibb Preparatory School On That Same Day. That Went According To Plan, At Least. The Fifth Grade Was The First Year Of Classes. My Mother Could Not Afford Morris-Knibb, So She Made The Difficult Decision To Send Dennis To An Elementary School Instead, Where He Would Be Boarded With A Local Family. My Mother Told Me That I Would See Him Every Two Weeks To Go To The Movies And Have Ice Cream. At Least Up Until I Was Nine Years Old, I'd Spent Time With Both Of My Parents. Dennis, At Age Five, Felt Abandoned By Both Parents And Would Never Get Over The Rage And Isolation He Experienced As A Result. He Would Be Tormented By It Until His Death From A Heart Attack At The Age Of 44. Our Mother Would Cry Every Time He

Did, Wracked With Remorse Over The Years That She Abandoned Him.

I Urged My Mom To Turn Around At Morris-Knibb And Take Me And My Brother Back To The North When We Arrived There. It Didn't Matter To Me Whether The Next Harlem Flat Was Tiny. I Didn't Mind That I'd Have To Do A Lot Of Babysitting. All I Wanted Was To Be In Her Company. To "Get Myself Together, Boy!" She Exhorted Me.She Showed Me Where My Bunk Was, And Assisted Me In Stowing My Belongings In A Little Locker. She Gave Me A Hug And Said Goodbye As We Walked Back To The Waiting Cab Outside. As The Cab Drove Away, I Saw The School Gates Shut Behind It. At Last, Utterly Broken, I Raced Up To The Gate And, With My Face Pressed Against The Bars, Howled My Anguish And Terror. However, The Cab Never Returned.

Back In The Classroom, My New Instructors Seated Me At My Desk. I Cried And Cried. That Night, I Didn't Feel Like Eating, And It Would Be Days Before I Ate Again. Then One Day I Woke Up And Realized I Could Get By On My Own. Nothing Could Erase The Reality That My Mother Had Left Me. Never Again Would I Expect To Find Affection From My Mom. I Had Become An Island Unto Myself. In This Cold And Impersonal Institution, I Was The Only Person I Could Put My Faith In. I Needed To Take Precautions To Avoid Becoming A Target Of These New Authorities. I Wouldn't Accept Whatever They Tried To Convince Me Of.

Mary Morris-Knibb Was A Major Player In Kingston And The First Woman To Be Elected To A Governmental Position In Jamaica. She Followed The British Style For Education, As Did Other Islanders. Even Though We Were Among The Many Nations That Britain Conquered And Ruled, We Learned British History And Etiquette,

Adopted British Accents, Read British Newspapers And Accepted Their Editorial Opinions, Followed British Sports Like Soccer And Cricket, And Swelled With Pride At Being A Part Of The British Empire After Watching Films Like The Charge Of The Light Brigade. Being Repressed Was The One Aspect Of Britishness We Disliked.

When It Came To Cricket, I Was The Odd One Out. This Was Hardly The Way To Win Over My New Professors And Students. It Didn't Take Much For Me To Get A Reputation As A Difficult Student, And I Often Received Canings For Infractions I Now Forget. While The Principal Lashed Me Across The Bottom With A Cane, Four Of My Fellow Students Grabbed My Arms And Legs. Even Though I Received Caning, I Never Turned Into The Docile Little Pupil That My Teachers Had Hoped For.

The Instructors Didn't Want To See Me Any More Often Than Required, So They Eventually Made Me Find Another Place To Stay. So I Moved In With Mrs. Shirley, Where I Shared A House With Three Other Guys. There Was A Room For The Four Of Us With Bunk Beds. My Mother Paid Mrs. Shirley A Weekly Stipend To Do This And Feed Me. It Was Too Much Money, Whatever It Was. Not Long After I Got Here, I Woke Up With Bites All Over My Body. Mrs. Shirley Made The Assumption That Mosquitoes Were To Blame The Next Morning Over Breakfast. "I Don't Think So, Ma'am. Mrs. Shirley Smacked Me When I Said, "I Think There Are Some Bugs In The Bed."I Returned To The Bedroom And Began Tearing Up My Bunk In A Fit Of Wrath While She Stood Silently Behind Me. Countless Bedbug Eggs Could Be Seen Clustered Around The Mattress Buttons. Mrs. Shirley Was Embarrassed And Told Me I Needed To Go.

For The Following Four Years, I Was Housed Not Out Of Love But Out Of Financial Need By A Rotating Cast Of Cousins And Acquaintances Of Friends. In Jamaica, Where One American Penny Was Equivalent To One Jamaican Dollar, Even A Fraction Of My Mother's Meager Wages Up North Went A Long Way Toward Covering Our Living Expenses. The Family Of My Mother's Sister Geraldine Stands Out In My Mind; She Had Practically Tahitian Skin, And Hers Was The Warmest And Most Welcoming. Aunt Gerry, Or Aunt G As I Knew Her, Married A Rosy-Cheeked Scotsman Named Eric Pigou (Pig-Ew), Elevating Her Already Lofty Social Position. At 17a Connolly Avenue In Kingston, In The Large Home Of The Pigous, I First Experienced The Rigidity Of Jamaica's Racial Inequality.

If Memory Serves, Mr. Pigou Was The Postmaster (Though There May Have Been More Than One). In Any Case, He Made Enough Money To Afford A Beautiful Two-Story Wood-Frame Home With A Tennis Court And Well Maintained Grounds. Phyllis, Violet, And David Pigou Are The Names Of The Pigous' Three Children, And They Are All As White As Their Father. Annette, Or Nettie, Was A Ward Who Had Been Adopted And Was Perhaps Six Or Seven Years Older Than I Was. Nettie Was Adopted And Had Mulatto Complexion, Therefore She Was Sent To A Tiny Bedroom In The Basement Of The Pigous' Home, Near The Rear Staircase. I Shared A Room With Nettie And Lived There As Well. The Pigous Kids Slept In Rooms That Were Considerably Bigger Than Nettie's And My Own On The Second Floor. Nettie And I Were Not Allowed To Leave The Kitchen When Visitors Arrived, So We Ate With The Staff Instead Of Joining The Pigous And Their Guests For Supper In The Dining Room. The Pigous Didn't Want Their White Pals To Find Out

That They May Have Dark-Skinned Relatives Living With Them. Later, I Would Find Out That The Pigous Were Hiding Something Much More Important From Me. Gerry's Daughter Nettie Was From A Previous Relationship. I Never Found Out Whether Mr. Pigou Knew This And Still Allowed Gerry To Keep Nettie Under His Roof, Or If He Didn't Know This And Thought Nettie Was A Ward.

Nettie And I May Have Joined The Others In The Dining Room Even Though We Weren't Asked. Because The Pigous Dined With Such Painful Formality, Their Backs Erect, And Every Piece Of Culinary Etiquette Rigorously Obeyed, We Really Preferred The Kitchen. At The Designated Time, We Picked Up Our Napkins, Gave Them A Little Shake, And Laid Them On Our Laps. We Sipped From The Spoon's Heel By Tilting The Outside Edge Into The Soup, Then Moving The Spoon Outward. So, There Was A Complete And Utter Escalation. The Pigous Spoke With The Same Pompous Air As Any English Lord Or Lady At High Tea, Carrying On Awkward Conversations In High-British Accents During Dinner (I Can Still See Mr. Pigou Turning His Spectacled Gaze To Me And Saying, "My Dear Boy, That Is Not What One Does At The Table"). Was It Really Just A Generation Ago That Aunt Gerry's Folks Threw From The Bonds Of Indentured Slavery, Only To Adopt The Mannerisms And Accoutrements Of Their Former Masters? Indeed, That's The Case. So Deeply Embedded Were These Pieces Of British Culture That The Pigous And Mrs. Morris-Knibb Had Taken, And Handed On, In Their Harsh Manner To Me, That In Less Than Twenty Years, People Who Encountered Me Would Believe I Was A Highborn College Graduate.

The World Outside The Pigous' Prim And Orderly Home Was Very Different. Peddlers Hawked Their Wares With Songs On Kingston's Crowded Streets. "Guava Jelly, Guava Cheese... Yellow Yam, Yellow Yam, Come Get Your Yellow Yam!"The Fishmongers Were The Greatest; Each Day's Catch Inspired A New Song. Tourists Disembarking From Cruise Ships Were Serenaded By Mento Bands Playing At The Port. Some Politicians Have Even Been Known To Sing Before Giving Addresses To Large Audiences. Simpson, A Politician, Had A Cork Prosthetic Leg, Which Prevented His Stump From Scraping Against The Wooden Peg. The Opposing Candidate's Song Included The Lyrics, "Cork Foot Simpson The Vagabon' / If I Catch You I Chop Off De Other One." Simpson Won, And He Sang His Counterargument At His Victory Rally That Same Night.

As I Walked By A Magnificent Hillside Mansion With A Vast Front Lawn Blocked Off By An Imposing Fence, I Took In All This Music And My First Snippets Of Classical Music. It Seems As If Whomever Lived There Spent All Day Listening To Bbc. The Static That Peppered The British Announcer's Voice Made It Seem Like His Signal Had Gone An Incredible Distance. I Climbed Up Into The Safety Of The Intertwined Branches Of A Bombay Mango Tree That Stood Sentinel Over The Road At The Property's Boundary. I Was Sitting In My Nest, Happily Sipping On The Nectar Of One Of Numerous Sun-Ripened Grapes, When The Sweeping Symphonic Waves Of The London Philharmonic Drifted My Way. I Heard Beethoven Conducted By Sir Thomas Beecham, Whose Name Alone Conjures Images Of British Grandeur And Splendour.

Regardless, I Felt More Alone In Jamaica Than I Ever Had In Harlem. I Was A Border Crosser, And I Had Black

Complexion, In The Eyes Of The Pigous. I Found A Kindred Spirit In Nettie, But Our Age Gap Prevented Us From Being Anything More Than Roommates. All Of The Older Pigou Kids Were Busy With Their Own Activities, And The Other Students At Morris-Knibb Preparatory School, Most Of Whom Also Lived At Home, Avoided Me As Much As Possible Since They Knew I Was An Outcast. Eventually, Mrs. Morris-Knibb Convinced My Mother That I Would Be Happy If I Transferred Schools, And Thus Started A Series Of Brief Spells At Schools Whose Names I Only Vaguely Remember: Mico, Wolmer's Boys' School, And Half Way Tree. Years Later, When Then-Prime Minister Of Jamaica Michael Manley Presented Me With An Honorary Degree From The University Of The West Indies, I Boasted That I Was The Only Person To Have Attended Each And Every School In Kingston.

I Did Have One Interest, And For A Time There, I Was Certain That It Would Become My Life's Work. I Used To Leave The Pigous' Home At Five In The Morning And Make My Way To The Kingston Racetrack To See My Cousin Charlie Gossen, The Greatest Jockey On The Island, Train His Horses. Liz, My Numbers-Crunching Aunt, Gave Birth To Charlie. He Became Well-Known In Jamaica As The Best Jockey Of His Time. The Man Taught Me To Ride After He Let Me Help Him With The Mucking Out And Grooming Of His Stables' Horses. We Thought I Had Potential, But Then I Went Through An Embarrassing Growth Spurt. Looking Up At Me Pityingly, Charlie Informed Me That I Would Need To Find A New Goal In Life.

Finally, In The Dead Of Winter In 1940, My Mom Picked Up My Brother And Me And Brought Us Home. Maybe It Was Simply In My Head That She Couldn't Take Being Apart From Us Any Longer. The War Was A Far Bigger

Factor. The Nazis Were Sweeping Throughout Europe And Seizing Nation After Country; France Was The Most Recent Victim. My Mother Wasn't The Only One Who Worried That England Would Be Invaded Next, And That The British Empire's Colonies May Fall Under Nazi Control Before She Could Get Her Boys Out.

My Brother Dennis And I Were Overjoyed To See Our Mom Again, And The Fact That Her Newest Apartment On 114th Street And Manhattan Avenue Consisted Of A Single Room Divided Into Two With A Shared Bathroom Down The Hall Did Little To Dampen Our Enthusiasm. My Sister And I Shared A Room With My Mom, And We All Slept On One Side Of A Homemade Curtain That Separated The Living Area From The Kitchenette And Eating Area. My Mom And Dad Got Divorced. They Were Devout Catholics, So Divorce Wasn't An Option. It Was Revealed To Me That My Father Had Begun Seeing A German Lady Called Edith. Though She Never Dated Anybody, My Mom Made A Buddy In The Building's White Janitor, William Wright. I Don't Believe It Would Have Shocked Me To Hear That He And My Mother Had A Romantic Relationship, Given The Way They Spoke Every Day. Bill Wright Would Soon Be Adopting Me And Becoming My Stepfather.

My Mother Was Keen To Find A Bigger Apartment Suitable For The Three Of Us And Move Out Of Her Little Room In Bill Wright's Building, Despite The Fact That This New Bond Seemed To Be Igniting Something. At 130th Street And Amsterdam Avenue, She Was Looking For A Neat And Tidy Building To Call Home. There Was Just One Catch: Non-Whites Weren't Welcome. My Mom Seemed Unfazed By It. She Claimed To Be Spanish When She Contacted The Rental Agency. Not Mexican Or Central American, But Rather European By Way Of The

West Indies — Specifically, Spain. We Used This And Another Twenty Dollars To Put A Down Payment On A House. But Now Dennis And I Could Say We Were Spanish, Too.

Now The "Passing" Phase Of My Life Had Officially Begun. The First Day I Hung Out At The Building, The Greek And Irish Youngsters Who Lived There Razzed Me On The Front Porch. "Hey, You're A Nigger," They Said In Shock.

"No, I'm Not," I Said. To Quote: "I'm Not A Nigger."

You Are Eerily Convincing As One.

"I'm Not."

That's How I Describe Your Hair.

Attitude Triumphed That Day, And The Victor Was The Phrase "Unless You've Been Caught In A Fire Like I Was, Shut Your Fucking Face." I Glared Them Down During The Awkward Pause That Followed, Having Learned The Hard Way That When You Don't Have The Truth On Your Side, Attitude Is.

They Believed Me Because I Kept To My Tale, And Also Because The Name Belafonte Added Some Spice To The Meal. After I Revealed That My Paternal Grandpa Was From Martinique And That My Ancestors Had Migrated To The Americas From Europe, I Was Quickly Dubbed "French" By My Newfound Friends. I Finally Felt Accepted Just By Virtue Of Not Being Black.

In This Mostly Irish And Greek Area, Where I Went To P.S., I Had An Advantage Over The Few Black Pupils Since I Was Frenchy. Public Junior High School No. 43 In The Area. I Sat With Several White Friends Of Mine For Lunch. They Would Invite Me To Play Stickball Or Basketball After School, And Because Of My Skills, I Was Always Picked First. However, The Newfound Friendship Could Only Go So Far. I Was Welcomed, But Only As A

Temporary Guest. I Didn't Belong To Their People. I Was Never Invited To Any Of Their Gatherings. Not That I Ever Even Considered Dating One Of The White Ladies. Even Though I Was Able To Strike Up Conversations With Them In The Halls Between Classes, If I Had Asked Any Of Them Out To The Movies, I Would Have Been Received With Real Shock, Followed By One Dishonest Anxious Excuse After Another.

So I Was An Outsider, A Cipher, A Hybrid Of Sorts, Existing Between The White And Black, The Big Apple And The Caribbean. That I Was Financially Disadvantaged Was A Given. That, Along With My Questionable Skin Tone And Peculiar Hair, Severely Constrained My Social Circle. The Son Of A Single Woman Who Worked As A Maid, I Was Of A Lower Order Compared To The Children Of Middle-Class Professionals Such As Butchers, Firefighters, And Construction Workers.

It Was A Difficult Period Of My Life, Marked By Isolation And Racial Uncertainty That Was Exacerbated By My Mother's Constant Attempts To Keep An Eye On Me. However, She Was Adamant That I Accompany Her To Every Political Event She Attended.

Her Political Opinions, Which Had Always Been Staunch, Had Become Only More Strident And Angry When She Was Unable To Improve Her Situation During The Depression. My Mother Looked Up To Black Nationalist Marcus Garvey, Who Was Born In My Family's St. Ann Parish In Jamaica With The Audacious Goal Of Reuniting Black People All Over The Globe With Their African Heritage, Marcus Garvey Founded The United Negro Improvement Association (Unia). To Unite The Whole Black Diaspora, He Advocated For A New African Homeland In Liberia, Complete With Brand-New

Educational Institutions And Economic Sectors, Much As The State Of Israel Did For Jews A Decade Later. In The Year I Was Born, He Was Deported From The United States Thanks To The Efforts Of A Young J. Edgar Hoover, Chief Of The "Anti-Radical" Branch Of What Would Become The United States Federal Bureau Of Investigation. Garvey Passed Away About The Time I Got Back From Jamaica. But His Legacy And His Vision Survived. My Mother Attended Garvey Gatherings In Harlem And Saw Him As A Ray Of Hope, But I Just Saw A Chubby Black Guy With A Goofy Admiral's Hat. My Mother's Respect For Garvey Had A Profound Impact On Me, And I Would Come To See That He Was, In His Own Way, A Pioneer Of The Civil Rights Movement.

My Mom Eventually Wed A Guy Named Bill Wright. Since Mother Was Expecting My Brother Raymond And My Sister Shirley Just A Year Apart, She Didn't Have Much Of A Say In The Matter. Unlike My Father, Bill Was A Kind And Compassionate Guy, And We Got Along Wonderfully With Him And My Brother, Dennis. Bill's Only Real Weakness Was That He Was An Alcoholic. But There Was One Thing Going For Him. He Was Completely Incapable Of Aggression, Unlike My Own Father. Since I Was A Lot Older Than Raymond And Shirley, We Never Became Very Close. (After I Saved Shirley From The Catholic Church, We Became Quite Close.) I Was Overjoyed For My Mom, Who Appeared To Be The Only One Who Couldn't Take Pleasure In Her Improved Situation. Poverty Had Crushed Her Spirit To The Point That She No Longer Had The Resources To Experience Joy. Even Though Her New Husband Loved Her Deeply, She Still Looked Doomed To Be A Troubled Figure Who Found Comfort Only In Religion.

The Shocker Was My Own Dad. When I Was Fourteen Years Old, He Had Changed Into A Completely New Person. On Friday Afternoons, I Would Take The Train To Lower Manhattan To Collect The Child Support Payment My Father Had Been Ordered By A Court To Provide To My Mother.

My Dad Was Still A Chef, But He Was On Dry Ground Now, Managing The Kitchen Of A Bustling Union Square Restaurant. He Was Too Busy Yelling Commands To His Subordinates To Have Much Of A Discussion. Despite The Pressures Of His Position, He Appeared Calm. The Delivery Of The Child Support Payment Envelope Did Not Dampen His Spirits. During One Of These Trips, He Introduced Me To Edith, A Waitress With A Loud New York Accent, A Stocky Build, And A Face That Could Cut Steel. My Dad Was About To Take Her As His New Bride.

After They Were Married, I Started Paying Them Periodic Visits In The Bronx. They Were Surrounded By Edith's Family, All Of Whom, To My Astonishment, Adored Edith's New Spouse. Like Me, Everyone Could See That He Adored Her. He Eagerly Completed The Menial Tasks She Assigned Him. At The Dinner Table, He Would Listen To Her Thoughts And Nod In Agreement; He Would Also Laugh At Her Jokes. That Imposter, Who Was He? And Why Did They Treat My Dad The Way They Did? This Could Not Be The Same Guy Who, At The Slightest Provocation From My Mother, Had Beaten Her Brutally And Then Me As Well. And Yet, He Was; There Was The Puzzle. My Mother Was The Most Lovely, Kind, And Always Right Person In The World, So Why Had My Father Been Won Over By This Plain, Powerful German Woman? I Was Well Aware That My Mother's Constant Nagging Had Played A Role, As Had Her Firm Belief That Males Were Inherently Foolish And Doomed To Let Her

Down. Perhaps It Became A Self-Fulfilling Prophesy For My Dad. However, I Soon Recognized That It Was Also Due To The Fact That They Were Both Drinkers. The Combination Of Being Young, Poor, And Intoxicated Was A Deadly One, And The Added Stress Of Being Illegal Immigrants On The Run Only Made Things Worse.

When I Was Fourteen, I Didn't Have To Worry About Becoming A Citizen. Although I Was Born Into Poverty, At Least It Was In The United States. It Was Everything Else, Beginning With My Identity, That Kept Me Up At Night. Inevitably, I Became Closer To The Black Pupils At George Washington High School Than The White Ones, And By The Time I Entered Ninth School, My Passing Phase Was Finished. To Join A Gang, Rather Than A Group, Was Now The Pressing Issue. Little People Of Midtown? Which Scorpions? Are They The Sharks? Who Are Those? Everything From Rocks And Knives To Chains And Brass Knuckles And Zip Guns Were Used In The Conflict. I Had My Choice Between Black And Hispanic People, But I Didn't Want Either. The More I Thought About Race And The More I Had To Battle For Myself Because Of My Race, The More Alone I Felt. Like You, I Found School To Be A Source Of Great Frustration. I Continued To Struggle With Reading To The Point That I Worried I Might Flunk Out Of High School Entirely. I Made It Through The First Half Of Ninth Grade Before Quitting.

When I Informed My Mom What I Was About To Do, She Was Heartbroken. The Expression Of Profound Despair On Her Face Is Seared Into My Memory. First, I Let Her Down By Not Practicing The Piano, And Now I've Let Her Down Again By Not Finishing High School. Daily, She Made Sure I Was Aware Of It. The Subsequent Year Or Two Left Me Feeling Lower Than I Ever Had Before. I

Worked Odd Jobs For Both Financial Reasons And To Get Some Distance From Her. I Worked As A Fruit Delivery Person And Grocery Runner For A Small Town Market. For A Short While, I Moved Racks Of Clothing Throughout The Garment District. Vincent Newby, My Adoptive Uncle From The Caribbean, Had A Tailoring Business, And I Worked For Him. I Was His Clothing Messenger And Quickly Picked Up Pressing Skills From Him. Finally, I Was On The Upswing! I Worked In The Press. With Any Luck, I May Even Be Able To Open Up My Own Tiny Tailor Business Someday. I Can Think Of Nothing More Ideal. A Lot Worse Things Have Crossed My Mind.

I Went To See The New Humphrey Bogart Film Sahara One Day To Take My Mind Off Of Things. The Black Actor Rex Ingram Really Captivated Me, Even Though I'd First Gone To See The Film For Bogie. Ingram Portrayed A Sudanese Soldier Who Joined Up With A Detachment Of Disoriented Allies In North Africa. The Plot Followed This Misfit Group As They Trekked Over The Deserts Of Libya In Search Of A German Unit. Ingram Chased Down A Nazi Officer And Shoved The Man's Face Into The Sand At One Point In The Narrative. The Camera Focused On Ingram's Black Hand As It Smothered The Nazi Soldier In The Sand Of The Desert, As Bullets Ripped Into His Body. Ingram's Act Of Vengeance Inspired Me Much. Never Before Had I Watched A Film With A Heroic Black Protagonist. For Sure, I Thought. For Me, This Battle Was Decisive,

When I Turned Seventeen On March 1, 1944, I Informed My Mother That I Wanted To Join The United States Navy. Many Other 17-Year-Olds Were Also Joining Up, Since They Just Need Parental Consent. The United States Had Committed To Fighting On Both Fronts Of

World War Ii, And The Tide Was Starting To Change In The Allies' Favor. From My Experiences Traveling To And From Jamaica By Water, I Knew That The Navy Was My Preferred Military Branch. Sailors Never Had To Slog Through Mud Like Army Troops, They Were Safe From Being Fired Out Of Aircraft, And They Got To Go To Sea, Which I Enjoyed.

As I Packed, My Mother Sat Quietly In The Living Room. She Hardly Got Up To Accompany Me To The Door. I Left Her With The Promise That I Would Return With Many Tales To Tell. I Didn't Know What Was Ahead, And I Definitely Didn't Suspect That One Day I'd Be Standing In Front Of An Audience With A Microphone In My Hand.

Chapter 4

I Was In Chicago, Illinois, About To Board A Train To The United States. North Of The City On The Shores Of Lake Michigan Is The Navy's Biggest Training Facility. It Wasn't Until Much Later That I Realized I'd Also Begun An Other Type Of Adventure At The Same Time. My Ability To Pass As French Was Long Gone. However, I Was Born In New York To Parents From The West Indies And Had No Notion Where I Fit In With The Majority Of American Negroes In The Middle Of The Twentieth Century. Despite My Exposure To Urban Poor, I Had Not Yet Encountered The Bitterness Of Discrimination. Like Haile Selassie's Disorganized Ethiopians Who Were Slaughtered By Italy's Fascist Troops, The Predicament Of Southern African-Americans Seemed Like A Faraway Concern. My Mom Supported Black Political Figures And Causes, And Selassie Was One Of Them. The Effects Of Southern Poverty And Racism On Me, As A Black Man In America And As A Citizen Of The United States, Were Not Yet Clear To Me.

At Naval Station Great Lakes, I Learned This The Hard Way When I Was Sent To An All-Black Camp Run By Robert Smalls, One Of Only 10 In The Whole United States (The Rest Were All White). Complex, Navy. It's Hardly Shocking That The Military Services Were Separated Back In 1944. The Diversity Of Black People In The United States Was A Shock To Me. Farmers In The Rural South Had A Thick, Rich Drawl That Required A Translator At Times. I Found A Bunch Of Northern Intellectuals To Be Just As Strange And Fascinating. However, I Was More Attracted To Them. I Could Follow Along With What They Were Saying, And Their Political Rants Really Piqued My Interest. Debate Persists Over

Whether Or Not African-Americans Have Any Place In This Battle. They Were Formerly Restricted To Low-Level Positions Like As Mess Attendants, Munitions Loaders, And Stevedores, With Practically Little Opportunity For Advancement. In The Minds Of Some, The Postwar Period Would Be More Welcoming To Minorities If Only Black Businesses Battled Bravely. Some People Laughed At Such Notion. All The Cynics Were Conscripts Who Had To Go To War Even If They Didn't Want To. They Were So Cruel To The Black Recruits That I Began Lying About My Age And Said I Was Drafted, Too. However, My Naiveté Was Exposed If I Ventured To Inquire More. How Did This Chihuahua Get Here?" Pondered One Of The Thinkers. They Threw Me Political Brochures Like A Dog Would Get A Bone, And I Started Reading Them.

W.E.B. Du Bois Was Often Mentioned In Such Leaflets. It Was Revealed To Me That In 1909, Du Bois, Black Educator And Scholar, Co-Founded The Naacp To Combat Racism And Prejudice. Reading About How He And Marcus Garvey, A Hero Of My Mother's, Had Become Fierce Competitors Was Fascinating. Du Bois Pushed For Integration, While Garvey Pushed For Separatist. Du Bois, The First Black Student To Get A Ph.D. From Harvard, Dreamed Of A "Talented Tenth" Of Black People Who Would Rise To The Top Of Government, Wall Street, And The Academic World Via Their Intellect Alone. Garvey Was Popular With The Working Class, Whereas Du Bois Was Seen As Pretentious By Him.

My New Barracks Mates Gave Me Dusk Of Dawn, Du Bois's Most Recent Novel, Which Is Also About The Struggle For African-American Independence. While Reading It And The Other Books They Allowed Me Look At, I Took Note Of The Many Citations To The Works Of

Other Academics. There Was One Person Who Was Mentioned More Frequently Than Everyone Else. I Rode The Train Into Chicago On My Next Day Off So I Could Visit The Public Library And Impress Those Black Thinkers There. I Was Able To Borrow Books Simply By Showing A Librarian My Dog Badge; After Reading Them, Military Members Could Return Them To A Designated Container On Base.

I'm Here To Assist, So Tell Me How."

The Lady At The Information Desk Seemed To Be In Her Early Sixties, Based On Her Peppery Hair, Rosy Skin, And Beautiful, Wide Blue Eyes. Perhaps She Was Mr. Pigou's Sibling. She Became Pale Upon Seeing The List Of Books I Want. I Had About A Dozen Titles Listed On Paper.

"That's Just Too Many," She Whispered.

"I'll Make It Easy, Ma'am," I Assured Her. Don't Hold Back; Give Me The Works Cited List.

She Glanced At Me. There Is No Such Author, She Said.

"Are You Positive?I Became Irritated.

She Said, "No, I'm Not Sure."

Please Have A Look At It If You Don't Mind." I Shot Back.

She Stopped Talking For A While, And In No Uncertain Terms Indicated That She Was Counting The Individuals Standing Behind Me.

"I'd Like To Find Out Before The War's Over," I Haughtily Responded.

The Librarian Nodded And Returned To The Card Catalog. The Ia-Ic Drawer Was Returned To Her. "Go Find Yourself," She Urged There Is No Citation Of "Ibid."

I Watched In Rage As Her Shoulders Slumped As I Fired Off A Few More Barbs. Ahead Of Her Reply, I Stomped Out Of There. After Returning To The Base, I Shared The News With My Companions. They Burst Out Laughing, Much To My Embarrassment. At Last I Got An

Explanation For My Monumental Error. "It's Just A Little Literary Shorthand," One Guy Commented Of The Practice Of Using "Ibid." Instead Of The Full Title Of A Source Book When Referencing It Again. Oh, Right. Feel Bad For The Librarian, However!

On My Next Vacation, I Returned To The Chicago Library, But The Tiny Elderly Woman Was No Longer There. I Found Out That She Had Volunteered Before. Hopefully, I Had Cured Her Of It. My Rantings Had Broken Her Spirit. That Day, I Waited About For Her, But To No Effect. After That, I Made It A Point To Walk Faster And Give Her A Sidelong Glance Anytime I Came Across Someone Who Resembled Her, Not Only In Chicago But Anyplace I Went. However, I Was Unable To Locate Her.

The Navy's Newest Recruits Were Given An Intelligence Test At The Conclusion Of Boot Camp. Test. My Academic Performance Exceeded Expectations, Surprising Me Much. Due To My Exceptional Knack For Organizing, I Was Selected For Training As A Naval Storekeeper, Or A Person In Charge Of The Navy's Supply System. I Boarded A Train To Hampton, Virginia, With A Group Of Other Black Men Who Wanted To Own Stores. We Moved Into Temporary Barracks On The Grounds Of Hampton Institute, A Historically Black Institution Established In 1868 On The Grounds Of A Former Plantation To Educate Freed Slaves In The Field Of Education. Even While The Institution Now Provided A More Traditional Liberal Arts Degree, Its Student Body Was Remained Entirely Black. Our Arrival Was Met With Lukewarm Enthusiasm, At Best. They Feared The Presence Of American Sailors Tarnished The Town Of Hampton's Scholarly Reputation. The School Administration Probably Agreed, But Hampton Had Benefited Greatly From Hosting Us "Gobs." For One

Thing, The Navy Had Constructed An Olympic-Sized Pool And A Sports Complex On Campus That Could Be Used By Both Students And Sailors. In Addition, The Navy Had Constructed Numerous Barracks, Classroom Facilities, And Other Buildings That Boosted The School's Reputation.

In Late August Of 1944, Before The Commencement Of The Autumn Semester, We Walked Across The Green With Our Duffel Bags Slung Over Our Shoulders, Our Heads Tilted Exactly So, And Our Gazes Fixed Ahead. All Of Us Had A Glimpse Of The Stunning Senior Coed As She Stood On The Mild Hill And Spoke To A Group Of Incoming Students. A Half-Circle Of First-Years Formed Around Her. She Walked A Few Paces Upward And Faced Them While Facing Us. The Student's Body Was Flawless, And Her Skin Was The Color Of Café Au Lait. And Her Hair Was Flawless As Well. My Mother Always Stressed The Importance Of Marrying A Lady With Nice Hair. Straight Hair Was A Sign Of Beauty At The Time. This Student's Shoulder-Length Hair Was Perfectly Straight And Shiny. I Knew She Was The One The Moment I Laid Eyes On Her. At That Moment, I Committed To Marrying Her. I Didn't Find Out Until Much Later That She Was The Campus Head Of The Anti-Sailors Group.

It Was A Long Process, But Eventually I Managed To Get A Date With Frances Marguerite Byrd. Sailors Lived In A Separate Section That Was Separated From The Students, And Our Higher Commanders Made It Obvious That Dating A Coed Was Not Allowed.

Like My Initial Encounter With Her, The Second One Seemed Distant. When I Was At A College Football Game (Hampton Was Part Of The Black College Circuit), I Saw A Chevrolet Convertible Slowly Making Its Way Around The Field. The Hampton University Crown Princess Sat On

The Ragtop With The Top Folded Back, Waving To The Onlookers. Similar Girl! I'm Sure I Picked Up Her Name That Day, But I Wouldn't Get To Really Meet Her Until The Next Campus Mixer.

The Administration Reluctantly Gave Its Blessing To The Socials Because They Wanted To Keep Sailors And Students Separate More Than They Wanted To Show Their Support For The Troops. There Was A Naval Band Playing All The Classics, And I Knew This Was My Opportunity To Shine; I'd Learned A Lot Of Dancing Moves In Middle School, And I'd Managed To Acquire Quite A Stack Of Records Despite My Lack Of Financial Resources, Which I'd Bring To Parties To Guarantee My Popularity. The Music Was At Home, But The Dance Skills Remained With Me. That Night, I Asked Marguerite Out On A Dance And She Said Yes.

As The Music Faded Out, I Told Her, "You Better Be Nice To Me."

"Why?"

"Because I Could See Myself Getting Married To You."

Margurite Was Taken Aback. "Why? Is There No More Males Left On Earth?" She Pronounced. But I Thought I Caught Sight Of A Glimmer Of A Grin Behind Her Frown.

After That, I Never Stopped Pursuing Her. After She Got Back From School, I Would Often Stay There Until She Went To Bed. I Was Never Aggressive, But Rather Amusing, And She Gradually Warmed To Me. She Was Standing In A Group Of Pals Outside Her Dorm With One Shoe Off Her Heel, Which She Was Balancing On Her Toes. I Realized That Was My Opportunity, So I Grabbed The Sneaker. I Was Expecting Her To Demand It Back, But Instead She Stomped Back Into Her Room, Barefoot On One Foot And Stockinged On The Other. That's Why I Decided To Keep It. Now Whenever She Sees Me, She

Inquires As To The Status Of Her Shoe. When She Went On A Date With Me, I Promised She'd Understand. She Finally Caved In.

After Overcoming One Difficulty On My Date With Marguerite, I Discovered That I Was Facing Another. She Was Born Into A Family Of Accomplished Individuals. She Intended To Further Her Education And Specialize In Child Psychology. All Four Of Her Brothers And Sisters Were Or Planned To Enter The Teaching Profession. They Had A Home, Not An Apartment, In The Suburbs Of The Nation's Capital's Capital.

What Does Your Dad Do For A Living?""I Decided To Inquire.

He Works In The Real Estate Industry.

The Real Estate Market, I Repeated. What Exactly Does He Do For A Living In The Property Market?""

He's With A Major Player In The Real Estate Industry.

Exactly What Does He Do For That Prestigious Real Estate Company, You Ask?"

He Is In Charge Of The Finances.

I Had Never Encountered The Segregated Middle Class Of African Americans Before. When The Byrd Family Moved To Washington, They Were Forced To Settle Into A Mostly Black Area, Send Their Kids To Predominantly Black Schools And Universities, Use Cabs And Bus Seating Reserved For People Of Color, And Take The Rear Of The Bus Themselves. But That Was Ok With Them. Marguerite Assured Me That Their Neighborhood Was Neat And Tidy, With Streets Lined With Attractive Homes; Many Of Them Belonged To Howard University Fraternities And Faculty Housing, Which Gave The Area A Distinct Air Of Campus Gentility Thanks To Its Ivy-Covered Brick Sidewalks And White-Columned Homes. The Public Schools Weren't Nearly As Outstanding As

The White Institutions, But Both Instructors And Students Had A Strong Motivation To Succeed Academically. Most Importantly, By Strictly Adhering To Segregation Rules, The Byrds And Their Neighbors Avoided Practically All Of The Everyday Racial Discrimination That Impoverished Southern Negroes Endured. From What I Could See, The Byrds Were Working On Their Own Version Of The American Dream Despite The Fact That They Appeared To Be Living In A Bubble.

I Realized I Was Far Outclassed In Every Regard (Society, Economy, And Education). So I Did What Seemed Like My Only Option: I Lied. Without Any Remorse, I Divulged To Marguerite That I Had Been Selected For A Top-Secret Mission Squad Trained By Admiral Nimitz Himself. What I Meant Was That It Included Submarines And Would Take Us Far Inside Enemy Lines, Where We Would Be In Continual And Deadly Risk. I Didn't So Much Win Her Over As Exhaust Her, And She Was At Least Somewhat Interested In My Stories, Whatever Fantastical They May Have Been. I Wondered What Wild Tales That New York Teen Would Dream Up Next.

When I Learned How Conservative Her Views Were, Our Dates Quickly Turned Into Heated Arguments Over Race. My Girlfriend And I Had An Ongoing Debate Over Whether Or Not African-Americans Should Resist Racism Everywhere They Encountered It (My Position) Or Give In To The Bourgeois Luxuries Of A Segregated Black Society And Hope For The Best (Her Position). Marguerite Was Unfazed And Unresentful Since Segregation Had Never Deterred Her From Pursuing Her Chosen Profession. Taking The Long View, She Believed That The Situation Of African-Americans In The United States Had Already Improved Significantly And Would

Continue To Do So Over Time. While Marguerite Never Managed To Calm My Rising Indignation About Racism, She Did Introduce Me To Some Excellent Reading Material On The Subject. I Felt Like I May Really Get An Education As I Fought Through Them.

After Four Or Five Dates, I Decided To Chance Telling Marguerite That My Purpose Had Been Shifted From Rescuing People To Giving Away Sweaters And Skivvies To Sailors. I Handed Her A Gold Locket To Ease Her Mind About It. I Was Shocked When She Said Yes To It. Then An Emergency Occurred.

Never In A Million Years Did I Think That Giving Blood As A Volunteer Would Get Me Locked Up In A Military Brig. A Lady In Hampton, Virginia, Was In Serious Danger When She Lost So Much Blood During Childbirth. The Whole Naval Force Was Alerted To The Urgent Need For Type-O Blood Donors. I Met The Requirements And, Along With Maybe Four Or Five Other Sailors, Proceeded To The Hospital. Unfortunately, Only Two Of Us Had Blood Types That Were A Perfect Match For The Transfusion. We Pulled Up Our Sleeves, But The Other Sailor's Circulation Soon Slowed To A Trickle. The Nurses Were Becoming Desperate, So They Asked If I Could Provide More Than Normal. I Did.

When I Finally Got Back To The Base, I Was Too Queasy To Do The Midnight Security Job For Which I Had Been Tasked. I Went To The Head Police Officer And Explained My Predicament, Asking If I Might Trade Shifts With Another Person. The Officer, A True Blue Redneck Cracker, Appeared To Take Great Delight In Telling Me That I Was Wrong For Donating Blood While I Was Supposed To Be On Guard Duty. The Dedication Of A Sailor To His Post Was Unwavering. I Sluggishly Made My Way To My Station. I Guessed Correctly That He Would

Stop By Somewhere Between Two And Three Hours Into My Shift To See How I Was Doing. "No Sleep While On Duty!"As He Yelled And Leaped From His Vehicle. To Put It Bluntly, "That's A Crime!""

I Didn't Say I Was Sleeping; I Said I Was Holding It Together.

"No Sleep While On Duty!" Please Report To The Captain's Mast Immediately.The "Captain's Mast" Was The Navy's Highest Court.

Instantly Enraged, I Screamed, "Why Don't You Go Fuck Yourself," And Cocked My Arm Back To Attack Him.

The Officer's Driver Overpowered Me Since I Was Too Exhausted To Put Up Much Of A Fight, And The Two Of Them Swiftly Detained Me For Assaulting An Officer. After Receiving A Two-Week Term, I Was Able To Stroll The Yard At Portsmouth Naval Prison With Many Other Incarcerated Personnel. A Large P Was Stitched Across The Back Of The Rough Denim Uniforms Worn By The Troops, Both Black And White. A Bigger Number Of German Pows Were Lounging In Another Area Of The Camp. They Won't Be Wearing The Jail Uniform. They Had Their Own Unique Outfits, Including Leather Bomber Jackets With Fur Collars. They Had Their Own Private Meals, Which Were Of Higher Quality. They Were Not Assigned Any Jail Work, At Least Not That I Could Tell. All Day Long, They Enjoyed Themselves In The Park. We Were Assured That Their Treatment Was Legal Under The Terms Of War. Not For One Second Did We Think That Was True. Nazis Who Had Committed Every Possible Act Of Murder Against American Troops Were There. But We Were Black And They Were White. I Was Revolted By The Unfairness Of It All.

I Was A Wanted Man By The Time I Got Back To My Barracks. Sadly, Marguerite Had Also Learned The

Devastating News. I Could See That Even After I Filled Her In On Everything That Had Happened, She Was Still Wondering What She Was Doing Hanging Out With A Sailor, And Especially One Who Was So Stubborn. Her Other Suitors Did Not Have To Worry About Being Placed In The Brig Since They Were Successful And Wealthy Guys On Campus.

Before I Could Put Their Minds At Rest, I Was Told To Get Aboard A Military Train And Sent Out To An Unknown Destination. After Giving Me A Quick Embrace, Marguerite Said She Would Keep My Locket. There Was A Chance That I Wouldn't See Her Again.

As We Rolled Westward, We Knew Where We Were Headed: Camp Shoemaker, The Massive "Fleet City" In The San Francisco Bay Area Where Up To 20,000 Sailors Prepared To Go On Combat Missions In The Pacific. We Expected To Be Placed As Storekeepers On Different Vessels And Subsequently Sent On A Journey To South China Or Iwo Jima. Instead, We Found Out When We Got There That We'd Be Living In The Port Chicago Neighborhood Of The City Of Fleets. In That Case, We Wouldn't Even Be Shopkeepers. Like Ravenous Beasts, Commerce Ships And Other Warships Would Gorge Themselves On The Live Bombs We Would Put Aboard Them. This Was Very Risky Employment, And We Had No Training To Prepare Us For The Risks We Were Taking. We Understood Completely Why We Had Been Selected. The Lowest And Least Important U.S. Sailors Were Assigned To Do Scut Task. These Are The Black Sailors.

On July 17, 1944, Not Long Earlier, A Massive Explosion Shook Port Chicago. 320 Sailors Were Killed And 390 Were Wounded When Live Weapons Exploded While Being Carried Aboard A Merchant Ship. Black Seamen Made About Two-Thirds Of The Total. There Were 258

Black Sailors At Port Chicago Who Had Refused To Relocate Weapons Following The Incident. As We Arrived On The Site, Which Was Still Littered With The Wreckage Of Buildings And Other Debris, The Sailors Were Being Tried For Mutiny And 50 Of Them Were Given Lengthy Sentences.

After The War, The Penalties Would Be Mitigated, But The Sailors Would Be Dishonorably Discharged, Lose Their Pensions, And Be Ineligible For Government Positions Because They Had The Courage To Challenge Systemic Prejudice. At The Time, We Just Did Not Know That. Nor Could We Have Predicted That The Political Fallout From The Port Chicago Tragedy Would Hasten The Desegregation Of The United States Military That Year (1948). The Sooner We Could Get Away From Port Chicago, The Better. The Good News That We Were Released From Our Obligations Arrived A Day Or Two Later. The Navy Was Already At Its Full Complement Of Black Munitions Loaders. Like A Reverse Newsreel, We Boarded A Train And Headed East To Yet Another Secret Destination. This Time We Surfaced On The Shore Of New Jersey, Near Naval Weapons Station Earle, South Of Staten Island. We'd Still Be Responsible For Keeping Live Ammo On Available For Munitions Loaders. The New Jersey Base, However, Had Not Yet Been Destroyed. And Asbury Park's Beach And Boardwalk Were Only Minutes Away.

Being Stationed Within Driving Distance Of Marguerite, Who Had Just Graduated From Hampton And Was Living At Home, More Than Made Up For Whatever Concerns I Had About The Work Itself. I Rode A Train To The Nation's Capital For My First Vacation And Could Not Contain My Excitement. My First Experience With Overt Racial Discrimination South Of The Mason-Dixon Line

Occurred When I Stepped Outside Of Union Station And Had To Wait In The Colored-Only Line For A "Colored Taxi." White Passengers Waited In The Station's Plushest Section, While The Colored-Only Line Was Located To The Side. When It Came To Public Facilities Like Restrooms, Theater Entrances, Water Fountains, And Wayside Motels, I Soon Discovered That "Colored Only" Signs Were Always Indicative Of A Less Than Stellar Experience. This "Colored-Only" Taxi Queue Was Ridiculous Since It Didn't Even Prevent Whites And Blacks From Using The Same Restrooms. Taxis Serving The Whites-Only Line And The Colored-Only Line Were Otherwise Identical; White Taxi Drivers, However, Had The Option Of Refusing To Pick Up Black Customers. Even If The People On Board Were American Soldiers Putting Their Lives On The Line To Defend The Country.

The Black Driver Affirmed That The Byrds' Home At 501 T Street Was A Very Excellent Location In The Center Of Washington's Black Neighborhood. Even Though I Was Leaving A Nice, Tree-Lined Neighborhood Where I Doubted I'd See Any Youngsters Shooting Marbles But Rather Riding Bikes, I Couldn't Quite Shake The Feeling That Something Wasn't Quite Right. The Byrds Shared Their Lovely Home With Another Family. Marguerite's Dad Could Be Good With Numbers, But Maybe Not For That Much Cash. Perhaps There Is Yet Hope For Me.

Marguerite's Mom Answered The Door, Welcomed Me In, And Gave Me A Thumbs Up For My Dapper Sailor Costume. "Hold On," She Paused It's A Threat: "I'll Get Her."

Marguerite Shone Brighter Than Ever Before. She Smiled And Appeared Happy To See Me, But She Didn't Get Any Closer. Soon Enough, She'd Be Warning Me That She Was Seeing Someone New—A "Jodi," As We Referred To

Civilians Of Draft Age Who Had Successfully Negotiated Deferments. Most Jodis Worked In The Defense Business Or Were Students With 4f Medical Classifications (Meaning They Were Ineligible For Military Duty Due To Conditions Like Allergies, Psoriasis, Homosexuality, Or Anything Else A Psychiatrist Was Prepared To Label Them As). They Had Managed To Avoid Direct Involvement In The Conflict. In The Following Months, Whenever I Suggested Visiting From New Jersey On Leave, Marguerite Would Notify Me That She Was Seeing Someone Else Named Jodi. I Saw It As A Hopeful Indication That She Still Had My Locket.

In New Jersey, I Spent The War's Last Months Helping Carry Live Ammunition Onto Cargo Ships From Underground Bunkers. I'm Satisfied That They Didn't Blow Themselves Up. We Would Go To Manhattan On Our Days Off In Small Groups Of Two Or Three, Find Dates Via Mutual Acquaintances, And Then Hit The Jazz Clubs. Dorothy Newby Was A Beautiful Young Lady, And One Night I Went Her To The Copacabana To Watch The Ink Spots. I Was Looking Forward To Setting The Table For Two With A Chilled Bottle Of Champagne. After Waiting Our Time, We Were Told To Step Aside By The Burly White Man Who Was Ushering In Couples One After The Other. How Are Things?After A While, I Asked Him. However, I Was Well Aware Of The Situation Before He Informed Me.

We're All Out Of Here, Buddy.

Why Are So Many Other Individuals Able To Enter?""

They're Set Up With Reservations.

I Glanced Back To The White Patrons Waiting In Line And Then At The Bouncer. Defeating This Son Of A Bitch Wouldn't Win Me Many Fans. To Get Away From What She Thought Was Coming, Dorothy Grasped My Arm.

Our Shame Was Deep, But The White Officer Who Had Been Watching The Whole Thing With No Apparent Empathy Told Me With A Chuckle That Putting A Black Sailor On His Arrest Report For The Evening Would Make His Day. Our Evening Was Ruined, And All I Could Do Was Sulk Off With My Companion In Shame And Frustration. I Had No Idea That The Copacabana Would Be Where I Got My Revenge.

On December 3, 1945, The Eighteen Months I Served Were Up. I Could Have Reenlisted Since My Civilian Options Were Limited, But I Had Grown Tired Of The Military, With Its Mind-Numbing Routine And Deadly Armaments, As Well As The Regular Instances Of Bigotry That Left Me In A Condition Of Nearly Continual Wrath. I Returned To Harlem, Almost Penniless, To Live With My Mom, Her New Husband Bill Wright, My Younger Brother Dennis, And My New Half-Siblings Raymond And Shirley. My Stepfather, Who Is Usually Kind, Hired Me To Help Him Clean The Buildings He Maintained. I Was Responsible For Cleaning Common Areas, Tending To The Heating Systems, And Fixing Minor Problems. Almost Instantly, I Fell Into A Depression Unlike Any I Had Ever Experienced. I Knew The Threats I Encountered In The Military And The Bigotry I Experienced Were Just Fleeting. From What I Could Gather, Janitorial Job Was My Future, And I Was Determined To Never Accept That Fate.

A Tenant In My Building In January 1946 Requested Me To Install Venetian Blinds For Her. She Tipped Me Two Tickets To A Show At The American Negro Theatre After I Completed That Menial Chore. She Told Me She Was An Actor And That She And Her Partner Were In The Play, Suggesting That I Would Like It. She Referred To It As The "Ant," And My Interest Was Piqued Despite My

Ignorance. Instead Of Going Out On A Date Since I Didn't Have Enough Money For Supper, I Went To See An Ant Performance At The Elks Lodge On 126th Street Off Lenox Avenue. I Went To A Play For The Very First Time That Night.

After Being Shown To My Seat, I Looked Out At The About Fifty Individuals Who Were Sitting In The Semidarkness Surrounding Me. They Had To Hush Their Conversation. The Apollo Theater, Vaudeville, And Movie Theaters Were All Places Where I'd Experienced A Distinct Atmosphere. There Was Usually A Commotion Or Some Joking Around Going On. The Room Was As Silent As A Catholic Cathedral.

When The Curtain Went Up And The Players Walked Out, They Had This Aura Of Spirituality About Them. Newly Composed, Home Is The Hunter Is A Drama By Samuel Kootz About African American Veterans Resettling In Harlem After World War Ii. These People Were Familiar To Me. The Issues They Were Facing Were Familiar To Me. It Wasn't Only Me That Connected With The Play. I Was Really Captivated By It. This Was A Brand-New, Thrilling Universe. My Tenants Clarice Taylor And Maxwell Glanville Were Onstage With The Other Performers. After The Lights Were On, I Was Simply Their Janitor, But After The Lights Went Down, I Felt Like One Of Them. Perhaps There Is A Way For Me To Contribute To This, Not In The Role Of An Actor But As A Mere... Assistant?

When The Lights Came Up And The Performance Was Over, I Remained Captivated In My Seat Until Everyone Else Had Left. I Mustered The Courage To Approach The Stage, Where Familiar Faces Were Being Greeted By Fans. I Was Timid When I Expressed My Delight In The Performance To Max And Clarice. It Was The Final Night

Of The Play's Brief Run, And As People Walked Up To Say Hello, I Saw The Stagehands Coming Out Of The Wings To Strike The Set. When I Saw They Needed Assistance, I Climbed Up On The Scaffolding And Braced To Assist. They Probably Thought I Was A Stagehand, Too, So I Stayed And Helped For Another Hour Or Two.

I Couldn't Sleep That Night Because Of My Excitement. I Couldn't Sleep For Wondering, "How Do I Get Possession Of This?" Over And Over Again. How Can I Integrate My Love Of Theater And These Individuals Into My Daily Routine?

The Next Day, I Went Back And Told Clarice And Maxwell How Much I Appreciated Their Performance. I Was Wondering If Anybody Was Available To Assist Move Some Heavy Pieces Of Furniture Over At The Ant. This Made Clarice Chuckle. Her Question Was, "Did I Hear You Say 'Volunteer,' Harry?'"

Answer: "Yes, Ma'am."

She Invited Him To Spend The Next Day With Her. Let Me Introduce You To Our Historic Preservation Office.

To Produce Plays "By, For, About, And Near" Black Audiences, As W.E.B. Du Bois Had Suggested, The Ant Was Founded In 1940 As A Community Repertory Theater In The Basement Of A Harlem Public Library Called The Schomburg. Slaves, Servants, And Butlers Dominated The Few Black Parts On And Off Broadway, With Some Gangsters And Prostitutes (Porgy And Bess), A Jealous Moor (Othello), And A Despicable Dictator (The Emperor Jones) Rounding Out The Cast. That's Why They Made The Ant, To Make Amends. It Was A Group Effort, With The Initials Suggesting That Members Would Collaborate Like Black Ants. Once A Piece Named Anna Lucasta Had Run At The Ant, Created Stars Of Its Actors, Most Notably Hilda Simms, And Made Its Way To

Broadway, The Goals Of Its Founders Began To Wane. The Other Members Of The Ant's Group Stayed In Harlem, Waiting For A Similar Break That Never Happened.

In 1949, The Ant Would Disband Amidst Acrimony. In January 1946, Though, It Still Had Some Life In It And Helped Start A Few More Careers. For Example, Clarice Taylor Would Go On To Play Bill Cosby's Mom, Anna Huxtable, On The Cosby Show And Appear In The Wiz On Broadway. After Acting In Movies (Cotton Comes To Harlem, Desirée), And Tv Dramas (The Iceman Cometh), Max Glanville Would Go On To Stage Manage And Direct Several Shows In New York. Not Me, But Another Guy In The Ant Who Had A Lot Of My Traits Became A Successful Actor Once He Ditched His West Indian Accent. We Were Approximately As Likely To Become Future Stars As Each Other; Sidney Poitier And I Were Both Scrawny, Moody, And Fragile Beneath Our Hard Shells Of Self-Protection.

Sidney Was So Reserved And Monosyllabic That I Mistook Him For A European At First. As A Group, We Were Once Rummaging Through Dusty Trunks Beneath The Stage In What Clarice Referred To As "Our Department Of Historic Treasures" To Find Costumes. Sidney Was Completely Silent. Those Were The Kind Of Individuals I Was Used To Hanging Around With; They Were The Lawbreakers Who Had A Lot To Conceal. Due To The Prolonged Lack Of Conversation, I Put Down My Costume Digging And Asked Him, "Sidney, Have You Ever Served Time?""

He Glared At Me In A Furious Hush. Wow! There Was Obviously Reverberation From Whatever I Had Brushed Against With My Quip. How Did You Come Upon That?", He Finally Said.

"I Didn't Pick It Up From Anybody."

And Your Point Is?"'"

After Staring At This Dark Mass For A While, I Changed The Topic.

I Wanted To Know Who He Was, And I Had A Sneaking Suspicion That What I'd Heard Could Be Genuine. Sidney Had Really Been Incarcerated Three Times. All Three Were Brief Stints For Minor Offenses Committed As Teenagers, Like As Robbing A Cornfield In Nassau. But These Were Really Embarrassing Truths About Himself, And He Was Shocked At The Prospect That They Had Leaked.

That Was A Rough Beginning. I Didn't Find Out How Eerily Similar Our Histories Were Right Away. Like Myself, Sidney Was Born In The United States (In His Instance, Miami, Florida), But He Spent The Most Of His Formative Years On An Island; In His Case, The Extremely Isolated Cat Island In The Bahamas, Where His Parents Made Their Home. Just Like Me, He Was A Misfit Who Grew Up Between Two Worlds, And He Was Furious. He, Like Me, Had Enlisted As Soon As He Was Able And Been Placed In A Black Company In The Military. His Time In The Service Was More Difficult Than Mine Had Been. He Had Almost Broken Down From All The Cruelty Directed Towards His West Indian Accent. When He Was Mustered Out, He Came To New York City As I Did And Worked Odd Jobs To Make Ends Meet. Sidney Was Trying Very Hard To Get Rid Of His Accent When I First Met Him; He Appeared To Assume That If He Didn't Speak At All, It Would Eventually Disappear. However, He Was Up Against A Far Greater Obstacle. He Couldn't Hear Nuances Of Tone. Any Black Actor Worth His Salt, According To The Ant's Stage Directors, Would Also Be Able To Sing And Dance. Sidney Failed At Both.

After We Got Over The Initial Awkwardness Of Meeting One Other, Sidney And I Became Good Friends. For Me, This Wasn't Just A Passing Acquaintance. Sidney Was The Very First Person I Ever Considered A Friend. Too Many Moves As A Kid Prevented Me From Forming Strong Bonds With My Peers. During My Time In The Navy, I Mostly Stayed To Myself, Engaging In Only The Most Surface-Level Small Talk With My Fellow Sailors. This Was Not The Norm. Sidney And I Were Supposed To Be Twins Separated At Birth; We Were Inseparable. It Was Easy To Predict What The Other Would Say Since Our Struggles, Disappointments, And Aspirations Were So Similar.

We Were Both So Financially Strapped That Talk Of Rapid Ways To Get Wealth Naturally Dominated Our Conversations. Sidney Intended To Sell An Aphrodisiac Conch Extract From The Caribbean. Perhaps It Also Had Substances That Helped Grow Muscle. Despite Its Potential, The Proposal Didn't Get Very Far Since We Needed Money To Implement It. We Then Settled On A Career As A Stand-Up Comedy Duo, With Poitier Joining Belafonte. We Spent Weeks Writing Material And Practicing On My Roof Before We Discovered Our Routines Weren't Hilarious. But As We Spent More Time Together And Discovered How Much We Had In Common, We Became Close. Once Or Twice A Week, We Began Sharing The Expense Of A Single Theater Ticket And Enjoying A Night Out At The Movies. We Would Take Turns Going In For The First Half, Coming Out At Halftime, And Handing The Stub And A Synopsis To The Other Person. That's How We Watched Several Live Performances, And We All Agreed That Even Missing The Second Act Of A Play Was Better Than Not Watching Any.

In The First Few Months Of 1946, Sidney Might Have Become Anyone: An Actress, A Comedian, A Successful Businessman. He Hadn't Gotten The Three-Month Trial With The Ant That He'd Hoped For After Bombing Out In His Initial Audition. He Had Begged And Pleaded To Be Permitted To Work As A Janitor At The Theater Throughout His Three-Month Trial, Just So He Could Feel Connected To Something He Cared About. It Was Winding Down Now, And Ant Director Osceola Archer Wasn't Keen On Giving Him Another Trial Run. According To Sidney, Osceola Is A Racist Town. She Had Long, Thick, Black Hair And Relatively Pale Complexion, Giving Her An Indian Appearance. Sidney Was Certain That I Was More Attractive To Her Since My Complexion Was A Lot Paler Than His. Nothing I Saw Indicated This, So I Assumed Sidney Was Simply Being Too Sensitive And Emotional. But More Than Anything Else, His Black Complexion Was What Gave Him Away As Different. It Made Him Feel Apart From Not Just White Society But Also Many Other Black Individuals.

Sidney And I Were Both Caught Off Guard When Osceola Asked Me To Join The Cast Of The Ant's Production Of The Farce On Strivers' Row. Unlike Sidney, I Wasn't Actively Looking For The Opportunity To Perform. My Favorite Part Of Working At The Theater Was Getting To Hang Out With All The Colorful Personalities While Getting My Hands Dirty With Tasks Like Setting Up And Tearing Down Sets, Changing Light Bulbs, And Pulling Ropes. I First Turned Down Osceola's Request To Audition For A Part Because Of This. I Flatly Refused To Get Involved, Saying, "No, No." I Never Thought I'd Be Able To Act. No Way Was I Even Close To Being Competent Enough To Attempt It. Osceola Continued Telling Me I Was The Appropriate Kind, And The Rest Of

The Cast Started Giving Me The "Group Muscle," So I Felt Like A Failure To The Whole Company. I Was Already In The Play By The Time They Finished Talking.

The Title Alone Told Everyone In Harlem What The Play Was About: The Wealthy Black Community Of Strivers' Row, Located Between Seventh And Eighth Avenues On West 138th And 139th Streets. The Play, Written By Abram Hill, One Of The Ant's Founders, Poked Fun At The Strivers' Social Pretensions, Which Came To A Head When The Teens Invited In Unsavory Characters As Houseguests. I Had The Little Part Of One Of The Kids, Which Made Me Feel More Like A Stagehand With A Handful Of Lines Than An Actor. The Collegiate Drama The Days Of Our Youth By Frank Gabrielson Followed, And I Was Cast In A Bigger Part, So I Must Have Showed Some Potential. Sidney's Three-Month Trial Period Was Passed, And Osceola Had Made It Clear That He Would Not Be Retained In Any Capacity Beyond That Of Janitor. However, She Made Him My Understudy As A Parting Gift. Obviously, Sidney Saw It As A Personal Slight When She Passed On Giving Him The Position And Instead Made Me The Backup.

I Was Becoming Cold And Nervous As I Read The Play. My Character Certainly Said A Lot! What Hope Do I Have Of Remembering Them All? I Doubled Back To Osceola And Begged Her To Release Me From My Obligation. This Was Becoming Ridiculous. The Stage Was Not For Me. I Would Just Bring The Show To A Halt. Osceola Grinned And Shook Her Head. She Said That At Initially, Everyone Felt The Same Way. Just Let Me Get Over It. Besides, I Wondered Whether I Really Wanted To Give Sidney The Limelight At This Crucial Time.

After A Tough Start, I Was Able To Enjoy Opening Night And Was Looking Forward To The Next Performance By

The Second Night. The Director Of The First Broadway Production Of Days Of Our Youth, James Light, Called Me A Few Hours Before The Special Performance Osceola Had Planned For An Audience Of One. The Person I'd Arranged To Take Over My Nighttime Cleaning Shift At My Stepfather's Building Was On The Line. There Was An Unexpected Conflict, And He Had To Cancel. I Even Offered Him More Than A Buck And A Half, But To No Avail.—Yet He Still Refused To Budge. Feeling Hopeless, I Hung Up. I Really Wanted To Play For The Famous Mr. Light, But I Had To Keep My 8:00 P.M. Commitment. Toss The Trash. I Was Responsible For Running The Dumbwaiter That Transported Trash Down To The Basement Every Night. Each Floor's Occupant Would Respond To My Doorbell Call, And When The Dumbwaiter Was Full, I'd Carry Down The Trash. The Trash Would Stink By Morning, The Tenants Would Be Angry, And I'd Be Out Of A Job I Couldn't Afford To Lose If No One Was There To Operate The Dumbwaiter. Disappointed, I Broke The News To Osceola That I Would Have To Miss The Concert. Now It Was Sidney's Turn To Shine.

As It Turned Out, Mr. Light Was Impressed With Sidney Poitier. Truth Be Told, He Came To The Ant Looking For Black Players To Fill Out His Broadway Production Of Aristophanes' Lysistrata. The Cast And Crew Would Be All Black. Sidney's First Stroke Of Luck Was Getting Cast In That Broadway Production By Mr. Light. His Follow-Up Was Much More Impressive. Even Though It Premiered To Terrible Reviews On October 17, 1946, And Closed After Just Four Performances, A Hollywood Representative Managed To Catch One Of Them. For The Lead In His Next Film, He Needed A Black Actor. The Film No Way Out, Directed By Joseph L. Mankiewicz And

Starring Richard Widmark As One Of Two Racist Brothers Who Have Been Injured During A Bank Heist, Was Sidney's Big Break In Hollywood.

In 1950, When The Film Was Released, I Watched It With A Mixture Of Astonishment, Pride, Jealousy, And Sadness. Whoops, I Had To Work As A Janitor That Night, And There Was My Coworker, Playing The Position I Would Have Gotten Otherwise. Thankfully, I Had Already Taken A Hiatus By The Time The Movie Came Out. But For Many Years After That, Whenever I Watched An Interview In Which Sidney Discussed His Meteoric Ascent To Fame, I Couldn't Help But Make Fun At Him. I'd Let Him In On The Secret Of His Success. Garbage And Its Demands!

After A Short Run In Days Of Our Youth, I Was Cast As A Young Irish Radical In Ant's Production Of Juno And The Paycock By Irish Writer Sean O'casey In July 1946. This Was My First Major Acting Role. It Didn't Worry Us That The Author And Its Protagonists Were Both White. We Could Relate To The Irish Farmers Who Stood Up To The British Because We, Too, Had Experienced Life In A Society Where The Victorious Were Stripped Of Their Liberties. The Play Was Written In Brogue, Which Was A Huge Hurdle For Me To Jump. Because Of My Illiteracy, I Took The Play Home And Worked Extremely Hard To Learn My Lines By Heart. To Calm My Nerves, I Kept In Mind That I Would Only Have To Give One Fairly Lengthy Speech, And I Tried My Best To Create My Own West Indian Take On The Accent. (The Other Performers Mostly Followed Suit.) After Seeing The Audience React To My First Words On Opening Night, I Was Eager To Go To Work. When Did I Get Stuck With Only One Lengthy Talk? For The First Time In My Life, When We All Took Our Last Bows, I Felt Like I Was A Part Of Something

Really Magnificent And Great. To Be Honest, I'd Never Been Happier In All My Life. Simply Said, I Wanted More. The Night Before Juno Opened, Rumors Circulated That Paul Robeson Would Be In The Crowd. This Was Unbelievable. We Was Really Impacted By His Presence. Why Was He At Our Little Harlem Theater, Anyway? Robeson Was The Black Deity Of American Theater, A Promethean Figure Whose Talents Were Unparalleled. That Was First Made Apparent During His Time As The Lone Black Student At Rutgers, Where He Excelled Academically, Participated In Every Varsity Sport, Was Inducted Into Phi Beta Kappa, And Graduated As Valedictorian Of His Class In 1919. He Treated His Career In Professional Football As A Side Note After That. By The Time He Was In His Mid-20s, He Had Starred In Every Major Play With A Black Main Character, Including Shakespeare's Othello, O, The Oriole, Eugene O'neill's The Emperor Jones, And All God's Chillun Got Wings. Robeson Began A Side Career As A Singer Of Folk Songs And Spirituals After Making "Ol' Man River" From Show Boat Into A Cultural Icon With His Amazing Basso-Profundo Singing Voice.

Robeson First Believed That As An Artist, He Should Stay Out Of Politics. However, When On Tour In Wales, After Performing To A Sold-Out Crowd, He Exited The Theater By The Back-Stage Alley And Saw A Group Of Striking Welsh Miners Singing To Collect Money For Their Families. Robeson, Swept Up In The Excitement Of The Occasion, Began Singing Along Enthusiastically. He Later Reflected On This Incident As A Watershed In The Politicization Of His Work. The Next Day, He Paid A Visit To The Miners In Their Houses, And He Has Never Forgotten The Miners' Plight Or The Plight Of Any Other Struggling Workers Wherever In The Globe.

By The Time The Spanish Civil War Broke Out In 1936, Robeson Had Already Began Criticizing The Fascist Regime Of Generalissimo Francisco Franco. When Adolf Hitler And Benito Mussolini Allied Themselves With Francisco Franco, Robeson Helped Fundraise For The Abraham Lincoln Brigade, An American Contingent That Joined The International Volunteer Army To Preserve Democracy In Spain. He Also Gained Notoriety For Making A Personal Trip To Madrid, Where He Stood In The Midst Of The Horror Caused By Hitler's Luftwaffe's Bombardment Of The City And Sang To The Liberating Troops. Robeson Felt A Deep Connection To The Underprivileged Of All Nations During This Period Of Worldwide Despair. That's Why He Identified With The Russian Proletariat And Socialist Ideas. Robeson Has Performed At Several War-Related Events During The United States' Involvement In World War Ii. More Recently, He'd Taken A Stand Against Racial Inequality In The Usa. Jackie Robinson Was Able To Break Baseball's Color Barrier In Part Because Of His Direct Approach To White Club Owners. When Southern Black Veterans Came Home From World War Ii Expecting Respect, They Instead Stirred Up The Homicidal Rage Of The Ku Klux Klan, And He Urged That President Truman Investigate The Wave Of Lynchings That Ensued.

I Looked Up To Robeson And Admired All He Achieved. There Is No Loftier Perch Than The One He Has Reached As A Complete Artist Who Uses His Voice To Protest Injustice. I Wondered How The Legendary Paul Robeson Would React To My Irish Accent, And I Was Prepared To Find Out.

After The Event, My Date And I Went Outside And Saw A Much Bigger Guy Than I Had Anticipated. He Beamed At Us And Said He Couldn't Wait To Tell One Of His Best

Friends, Sean O'casey, How We Black Performers Were Faring In New York With His Play. Robeson Assured Us That Our Production Of Juno Was Excellent. Success Was Shared Between Everyone. But What He Truly Liked Was That We, A Black Repertory Company, Had The Guts To Do This Play In The First Place, Despite Its High Production Costs, Challenging Dramatic Arc, And White Author/White Character Cast. Robeson Was An Avid Supporter Of The Ant's Efforts To Develop And Showcase The Work Of Black Playwrights. But, He Lamented, There Were Still Very Few Outstanding Black Plays To Be Discovered. Therefore, We Should Not Just Tackle Plays By Black Writers Like Zora Neale Hurston, Langston Hughes, And A Limited Number Of Others, But Also Works By White Playwrights Like John Steinbeck, Clifford Odets, And George Bernard Shaw Who Depicted Societal Themes That Affect Us All. There Was A Lot Our Theater Could Do To Spread Awareness And Understanding Of Those Topics, So We Had To Do All In Our Power To Make It Thrive.

We Listened In Awe, Too Overjoyed To Say Anything. More Than His Words, Robeson's Affection And The Deep Obligation He Felt As Black Actor To Utilize His Position As A Bully Pulpit Are What I Remember About Him. Acting On A Harlem Basement Stage Was Not Something I Thought Would Go Anywhere. But I Knew I'd Discovered My Inspiration, And My Perspective On The Stage Would Never Be The Same Again. Every Day When I Woke Up, My Mom Would Remind Me To Plan Out How I Would Fight Against Injustice. My Life-Changing Realization Came To Me That Night While Listening To Paul Robeson.

At The Time, I Lacked Both The Courage And Resources To Pursue Marguerite. This Was Particularly

Disheartening Since She Had Finally Settled Into Adult Life With A Job In New York After Graduating From Hampton And Moving Back In With Her Parents. While Applying To New York University For A Master's Degree In Teaching, She Planned To Work At The Bethany Day Nursery, A Prestigious Day Care In The East Thirties, And Live In The Teachers' Dormitory Next To The School. As Soon As She Was Settled In, I Paid Her A Visit. I Got The Impression That She Was Glad To See Me, But That I Was More Of An Exotic Friend To Her Than A Love Interest. My Sudden Interest In Acting Was A Source Of Real Concern To Her. A Rent Check Wouldn't Come From Performing. Insanity, What Madness Was This? Her Skepticism Did Nothing To Weaken My Determination.

It Seemed Reasonable To Pursue A Career In The Arts If I Wanted To Impress Marguerite And Give My Life Some Significance. I'd Heard That A German Emigre Director Had Set Up The City's Most Fascinating Theatrical Workshop At The New School For Social Research In The City's Downtown. It Was The Topic Of Conversation Between All Ant Patrons. The Best Part Is That The G.I. Bill Would Pay For My Schooling. Marguerite Was Really Irritated By That. I Can't Believe I Considered Wasting My Gi Bill Benefits On... Theater Lessons.

I Braved The Interview Nevertheless. Yes, The School Would Take Money From The G.I. Bill, And Yes, I Could Enroll In The Dramatic Workshop (Or Whatever They Called It). My Argument Began In Earnest. How Could The New School Allow A Little Detail Like That To Prevent Such A Skilled Performer, A Seasoned Veteran Of The American Negro Theatre, From Attending? My Interviewer Told Me To Hold My Tongue; I Would Need To File A Formal Appeal With The Workshop's Board. I Arrived At The Scheduled Hour To Find Four Judges

Already Waiting. The One That Stood Out The Most Had Pink Complexion, A Shock Of White Hair, And Piercing Eyes. His Dialect Was German, And He Carried Himself With A Severe Prussian Air. The Name Of The German Director And Workshop Founder I Had Heard Of Was Erwin Piscator. My Goal Should Have Been To Win Him Over. I Was Aware Of His Socialist Leanings And Used It To My Advantage By Portraying Myself As A Victim Who Was Pressured Into Dropping Out Of School. In Painting This Image, I Admit To Have Bent The Facts A Little Bit To Make It More Dramatic. However, The Intended Result Was Achieved.

Perhaps The Board Thought Adding An American Negro Or Two Would Be A Good Idea. When I Arrived On My First Day Of School, I Was The Sole Student In My Class Since The School Had None. My Classmates And I Each Introduced Ourselves To The Group. Marlon Brando, Rod Steiger, Wally Cox, Elaine Stritch, Walter Matthau, And Bea Arthur. Tony Curtis, Formerly Known As Bernie Schwartz. I Didn't Give Any More Weight To Their Names Than They Did To Mine.

Piscator's Was The Only Name That Really Stuck Out. He Was A Titan Of German Theater In The Twentieth Century, And His Harrowing Experiences In The German Troops During World War I Informed His Work. His Solution To The Follies Of War Was To Become A Member Of The Dadaist Movement And Stage Plays That Embraced The Dadaists' Theme Of Silliness And Formlessness. After Realizing That Dada Was Reaching Its Limitations, He Established A Communist Theater In Berlin, Where He Performed Works By Maksim Gorky And Others In Workers' Halls, With Free Admission For The Jobless. The Plays Were Dramatic Depictions Of Contemporary Political Topics, And They Used Innovative

New Visual Components That Communicated Directly To The Audience, Such As Information Flashing On A Tiny Side Screen While The Performers Delivered Their Lines Or Combat Video Presented Behind Them. Since These Elements Served A Similar Informational Function To That Of A Greek Chorus, Piscator And Bertolt Brecht Dubbed Their Method "Epic Theater." After Being Forced To Travel To Moscow As A Political Exile Because Of Hitler's Ascension To Power, Piscator Eventually Made His Way To Paris. In 1939, As Hitler Prepared To Invade France, Piscator Sought Refuge From The Political Climate Of The United States And Found It At The New School. One Of The Most Interesting And Important Theatrical Ventures In American History Had Its Beginnings At This Time.

The Legendary Filmmaker Never Taught Any Acting Workshops. I Sat In On His Classes, But The Only Times I Got A Good Look At Him Were When He Rushed By Me In The Corridors. I Was Well Aware That Mr. Piscator Was Not One To Be Interrupted During Serious Conversation. His Enthusiasm And Sense Of Purpose Filled The Session, And It Energized And Motivated Everyone There. Drama Was Taken Very Seriously; It Was Used As A Means To Expose Corrupt Authorities, Effect Social Reform, And Highlight The Futility Of War. At The Dramatic Workshop, You Won't Find Any Screwball Humor Or Light Stuff. And Theoretically Speaking, No Stars. In Piscator's Dramatic Collective, We Were All Treated As Equals On The Job. In This Spirit, We Studied Not Only The Art Of Acting, But Also That Of Creating Sets, Operating Lights, Directing, And Writing Plays. In One Play I May Play A Role, While In Another I Could Be In Charge Of Lighting. We Wrote Several Of Our Plays As A Group. But Piscator's Fame Also Resulted In

The Production Of Works By Established Authors. During My Time There, The Workshop Staged The First American Production Of The Flies, And Jean-Paul Sartre Himself Attended The Opening Night. The Pulitzer Prize–Winning Book All The King's Men Was Adapted For The Stage For The First Time By Robert Penn Warren. Motivated, I Went On To Read All The Classics I Could Get My Hands On, In Addition To These Plays And Every Other One Piscator Had Recommended. My Whole Universe Expanded In Those First Few Months At The Dramatic Workshop. My Relocation To The Village Followed My Enrollment In The Course. Living With Her And Her New Family In A Small Harlem Apartment Had Put Me And My Mother On Edge, And I'm Sure It Did The Same For Marguerite When She Found Out I'd Spent My G.I. Bill Money On Theatrical School. Until I Could Find My Own Home, Ant Director Charles Sebree Let Me Stay For Free In His Bleecker Street Apartment. Charles Was Homosexual, And He Hoped That He And I Might Make The Transition From The Living Room To The Bedroom. That Was Uncomfortable. As Soon As I Could, I Arranged For A More Suitable Arrangement With The Help Of Alan Greene, A Fellow Composer And Ant Employee. In The 1980s, Alan Shared A Spacious Basement Flat On Central Park West With Another Lyricist. They Had A Really Decent Show, And They Both Played The Harmonica. My Proposed Monthly Payment Was $9.50, Which Was Less Than A Third Of The Total Rent. They Suggested That I Make Up The Difference By Acting As The Group's Chief And Cleaning Guy. To Fund This Endeavor, I Once Again Sought Out A Part-Time Job In The Garment Area, This Time Moving Racks Of Clothing.

My New Housemates Were Both White, So I Suppose I Looked A Little Bit Like Some Kind Of Black Retainer

When I Offered To Cook And Clean For Them. And Yet, It Didn't Happen. There Was No Longer Any Racial Divide In My Mind. Whenever I Was Around White People, I Braced Myself For The Next Unconscious Racist Slight, Like The White Woman Who Tensed As I Entered The Elevator And Clutched Her Handbag More Tightly Under Her Arm, Or The White Man In A Suit And Tie Who Spoke In What He Thought Was Black Lingo To Demonstrate His Liberalism. In This Place, None Of It Existed. Alan And His Roommate Were Both Open-Minded And, Not Surprisingly, Staunch Democrats.

Politics Was A Topic Of Conversation Across All Of Postwar Manhattan, But Notably On The West Side And In The Village. The Differences Between Socialism, Communism, And Progressivism Were Not Obvious In 1947, When I Was A Political Novice. Long Conversations On How To Make The World A Better Place Were Fuelled By Cheap Wine And Liquor At Parties. Writers Like John Steinbeck And Ernest Hemingway, Playwrights Like Arthur Miller And Clifford Odets, And Even Poets Like Dylan Thomas Were All Writing And Openly Discussing How To Change Capitalism, And Russia, Still Our Partner In The Win Over Hitler, Looked To Be At The Forefront Of This Movement. Race Was A Major Factor In All Of This: No Of The Specific Utopian Ideal Being Advocated, All People Everywhere Would Be Treated With Respect And Dignity Regardless Of Their Ethnicity. I Attended Classes At The Jefferson School On Sixth Avenue, Which Proudly Declared Itself To Be A Center For Marxist Study With Ties To The American Communist Party. I. F. Stone, A Journalist, Spoke At One Of Them, As Far As I Recall. Young Lefties And Hard-Core Workers Mingled During Lectures Held In Union Halls. Both Socialists And Communists Saw The Working Class As Essential To The

Establishment Of A New Political System. They Promised To Repeal The Federal Government's Strike-Breaking Legislation. The Atmosphere Of Fraternity That Was Fostered In Such Gatherings Was Appealing To Me. Although I Had Certain Sympathies With Communism And Socialism, I Never Joined Either Party In The United States And Never Considered Myself A "Fellow Traveler," As The Lingo Of The Time Put It. Perhaps The Thought Of Joining Anything Kept Me On The Outside. Only The United States Navy Had A Political Objective, And I Was Relieved To Be Free Of That Organization.

I Enjoyed Spending Time With Tony Curtis. He And His Family Were Bronxites Because, As He Often Put It, "Why Live Downtown When You Can Live Uptown For Free?" And It Didn't Matter Whether He Was Still Addressed As Bernie Schwartz When He Got To The Top. Tony Didn't Need To Live In The Village To Show How Brilliant He Was Or How Gorgeous He Was; He Already Knew. We Socialized Extensively At Various Gatherings. Sometimes We'd Go With Bea Arthur And Elaine Stritch, Who Would Start Matching Wits Till They Had The Whole Place In Fits Of Laughter, And Elaine Would Swear More Colorfully Than Any Sailor I'd Ever Known. They Made A Stunning, Sizzling, And Lively Duo: Bea, The Brash Jewish Comedian, And Elaine, The Diva. Even Though Walter Matthau, A Resident Of Hell's Kitchen, Was Great Company, He Still Preferred Betting On Horses Over Attending Social Events. At Least Three Jowly-Looking People In Raincoats Came To See Him At School Once, And I Remember It Well Because He Owed Them Money.

However, There Was One Student In Particular Who Everyone Wished They Could Sit Next To Every Day: Marlon Brando. In The Autumn Of 1947, Brando Was

Already Well-Known As A Stage Actor, Thanks In Large Part To His Dark Portrayal Of A Damaged Soldier In Maxwell Anderson's Truckline Café, For Which He Was Dubbed "Broadway's Most Promising Actor." Then He Starred With Paul Muni In A Flag Is Born, A Play That Openly Advocates For The Establishment Of A Jewish State In Palestine, And He Co-Starred With Katharine Cornell In Her Newest Production Of George Bernard Shaw's Candida. Now, He Was Going To Be The Main Character In The Stage Adaptation Of A Streetcar Named Desire. He Had Never Been A Regular Student At The Dramatic Workshop, And Now That Rehearsals Were Underway For Streetcar, He Was Even Less Likely To Show Up.

Whether Or Not Marlon Was Present In Class, He Had A Significant Effect On Us. Without Without Realizing It, We All Started Channeling Our Inner Marlon Brando. When He Did Show Up To Class, It Was Always With An Abundance Of Emotion, And No One Could Predict Whether That Feeling Would Be Happy Or Sad. Then, I'd Sometimes Hop On His Motorcycle With Him, Bareheaded Of Course (No One Wore A Helmet Back Then, At Least No One Remotely Cool), And Holding On For Dear Life As He Roared Down The Streets Of The Village With His Cycling Soul Mate, Wally Cox. I Was Ready To Join This Cult By Purchasing My Own Bike When I Stopped To Give It Some More Thinking. My Innate Survival Instinct Triumphed Over My Need For Social Acceptance.

Marlon And I Quickly Learned That We Had A Common Background: Our Family Had Both Struggled With Alcoholism. A Strong Relationship Was Formed There. We Shared Stories About Our Alcoholic Dads And Learned To Speak Each Other's Lingo. We Also Quickly

Established Our Shared Preference For Female Company. Which Is To Say, We Had A Lot Of Female Crushes. That Constant Need For Validation And Affection Probably Stems From Our Alcoholic Parents. We Knew We Were Above Average, To Be Quite Honest. Finding Ladies Didn't Take Much Effort On Our Part. We Had People Come Seeking For Us.

Double Dating Between Marlon And I Became Commonplace Quite Quickly. Never Before Had I Seen A White Guy Who So Enthusiastically Celebrated Black Heritage. He Was Always Down To Accompany Me To Jazz Venues. Between Performances, I Would Often Strike Up Conversations With The Black Musicians, And I Was Able To Introduce Marlon To Them. Eventually, He Wouldn't Need My Assistance, But Just Then, Before Streetcar Opened, I Was His Ticket. Marlon Preferred Black Ladies Over Black Artists. My God! The Katherine Dunham Dance Company Had A Plethora Of Attractive Women, So He Signed Up For Drumming And Dance Lessons With Great Enthusiasm. He Was A Huge Fan Of The Legendary Cuban Percussionist Chano Pozo, Whom He Admired Much. I'm Sure He Slept With A Few Of His Fellow Drum Majors, But Julie Robinson Was His Main Interest. I Didn't Know That At The Time, But I Did Get To Watch Julie Perform At The New School With A Few Other Dunham Dancers. I Couldn't Help But Fall For Her Slim, Alluring Body. But I Never Got To Meet Her In Person. When We First Started Dating, I Had No Notion That We Would Eventually Get Married.

Marlon Was A Joker Who, Among Other Things, Would Knot Your Shoelaces Together If He Caught You Asleep. More Than Time, We Did It To Each Other. However, He Was An Unwaveringly Faithful Buddy. I Met Up With Him To Go To A Black Nightclub In Los Angeles Not Long After

Our Professions Brought Us There. A Raid Occurred While We Were There. Customers Were Being Herded Against The Wall, Frisked, Handcuffed, And Herded Into Paddy Wagons At Gunpoint. The Film Adaptation Of Streetcar Had Been Out At This Time, So The Cops Were Familiar With Marlon. They Ushered Him Away And Whispered Instructions To Go Out The Rear Exit. To Which I Replied, "I've Got A Friend With Me," And He Pointed To Me. No One Knew Who I Was Since I Hadn't Yet Become Famous. An Irritated Police Officer Told Marlon, "Look, You Should Consider Yourself Lucky That We're Letting You Out On Your Own." Marlon Shook His Head Firmly. "I'm Afraid Not; I Can't Go Without Him." The Officers Were So Frustrated That They Finally Let Us Leave.

The Awful News Arrived Now From Marguerite. There Were Intense Romantic Feelings Between Her And A Black New York Times Writer. She Liked Me And Wanted To Meet Me Again, But She Also Returned My Necklace Since She Didn't Want To Keep It. My Professional And Marriage Prospects Were Looking Dismal While I Was Still Moving Racks Of Garments In The Garment Area. But I Still Hoped That Things Would Turn Around If I Landed A Major Part And Managed To Charm Marguerite Into Marriage. That's Why It Was A Relief To Me That She Wasn't Wearing An Engagement Ring. Still Still Space To Maneuver, I Reasoned.

The Director Of The Bethany Day Nursery, A Tall, Extremely Ivy League-Sounding Lady Called Mrs. Bears, Turned Out To Be An Unexpected Ally. It Turns Out That She Shared My Political Leanings Toward Progressivism. She Pursed Her Lips In Approval As I Told Her About Recent Union Meetings I'd Attended And My Plans To Help Henry Wallace, The Presidential Candidate For The

New Progressive Party, Win The Election. I Could Sense Marguerite's Confusion As She Tried To Process The Fact That Her New Employer Shared My Outlandish Political Ideas.

During Marguerite's Update On Her Siblings' Recent Academic Achievements, Awards, And Job Offers, She Managed To Squeeze In A Tidbit About Her Father That Really Surprised Me. The Money For That Swanky Real Estate Law Practice Was Still Being Handled By Mr. Byrd. His Actual Work, However, Was Not What She Had Intimated. The Legal Company Used Him As A Handyman. The Maid! He Maintained The Peace And Order! One Of His Responsibilities Was To Deposit The Cheques For The Previous Week At The Bank Every Friday And Bring Back The Deposit Slip. That's How Much Cash He "Handled."

Here I Learned More About The Inner Workings Of The Ostensibly Prosperous Black Middle Class In America. The Black Middle Class Exists In Isolation, With Its Own Distinct Stratifications. Mr. Byrd Had To Pretend He Belonged Among The Attorneys, Physicians, And Accountants Of The Middle Class In Order To Be Accepted By Them. His Offspring Were Also Obligated To Lie To Their Peers On His Behalf, Whether They Realized It Or Not. There Was Truth To Some Of The Stories Marguerite Told Me About Her Ancestors. Even If Some Of The Cost Was Covered By Scholarships, Her Father's Accomplishment Was Still Noteworthy. And He Did Keep Up The 501 T Street Residence. However, He Was Not The One Who Really Handled The Money.

One Was A Vast, Old Yiddish Theater On East Houston Street That We Named The Rooftop, And The Other Was A Smaller, Better-Equipped Uptown Theater On Eighth Avenue And Forty-Eighth Street Where We Produced

Our Most Ambitious Performances. Marguerite Attended Both Performances, But She Still Doesn't See Where All Of This Acting May Go Me. Uptown Was My Favorite Of The Two, And I Often Helped Out Backstage By Operating Lights And Props When I Wasn't Cast In A Part. Manual Labor Was Still Appealing To Me. Even Better, Following The Curtain Call, I Enjoyed Visiting The Royal Roost, One Of The Finest Jazz Clubs In New York City's History. Marguerite Didn't Care Much For Jazz, So I Was Very Much On My Own When I Went To The Roost. The Well-To-Do Occupied Tables And Placed High-Priced Drink Orders. I Hung Out At The Rear Bar, Separated From The Crowd By Glass, Where I Could Purchase A Drink For A Buck And Listen To The Likes Of Charlie Parker, Ella Fitzgerald, Miles Davis, And Lester Young For As Long As I Pleased. After Establishing Rapport With The Wait Staff, I Was Sometimes Upgraded To A Front-Of-The-House Seat When Business Was Sluggish. Only Fifty Cents For The Finest Jazz In The World! It Felt Like I'd Died And Gone To Paradise. Later, I Started Making An Effort To Socialize With The Performers In The Breaks Between Their Acts, Whether By Buying Them A Beverage Or Just Listening To Them. The Harsh Economy, National Or International Politics, Racial Tensions, And, Of Course, Joe Louis's Recent Fight And Jackie Robinson's Prospects As A Rookie With The Brooklyn Dodgers Were All Topics Of Conversation. However, The Most Of Their Conversations Was On The Music They Listened To And The Artists They Knew, Namely The Drug Or Relationship Problems That Each Individual Was Experiencing.

Lester Young, The Great Tenor Saxophonist Whom Billie Holiday Had Dubbed The "Pres" For His Superb Playing And Perfect Composure, Was My Favorite Of The Bunch.

An Example Of How Awesome Lester Was: The Term Was His Own Creation. It Was Part Of A Code He Spoke With His Buddies And Musicians Exclusively. The Player's Keys, Or His Fingers, Were His "People," And A "Molly Trolley" Was A Practice Session (Or A Rehearsal; "Does The Bread Smell Good?"). Lester's Resume Included Stints With The Likes Of Fletcher Henderson, Andy Kirk, And Count Basie. He Has Supported Such Artists As Nat King Cole And Billie Holiday. Recently, He Began Touring With Norman Granz's Ever-Changing Jazz At The Philharmonic Ensemble, Which Originally Debuted At The Philharmonic And Continued To Use The Name Even After Granz Took It On The Road. In Between Philharmonic Dates, He Occasionally Performed At The Roost With A Backup Band That Featured Charlie Parker, Miles Davis, And Pianist Al Haig. Many Jazz Fans, Including Myself, Had Already Crowned Him The Finest Saxophonist In The World By 1948.

Lester Socialized In A Small Group. Given The Quantity Of Cocaine They Used Offstage, Lester And His Bandmates Had Cause To Worry That An Outsider Would Turn Out To Be A Narcotics Detective—A "Bob Crosby," In Lester's Private Terminology. Even If They Weren't, A Random Person Was Probably Not Cool. When Lester Turned To Me Between Sets And Said, "What Is It, Exactly, That You Do?" I Wasn't Sure Whether He Was Welcoming Me Or Confronting Me.

I Introduced Myself As A Student. One Who Studies Theatre As An Academic Discipline.

Which Branch Of Drama Do You Major In?"

I Told Him I Was Acting.

Then, After A Little Gap During Which His Previous Cocaine Snort Could Clear His System, He Said, "And How Do You Do That?"

This Is A Question I've Never Been Asked Before And I Still Don't Know The Answer To. I Assured Him We Were Putting On Excellent Performances, So I Guessed That Helped.

When Asked, "How Do You Know They're Good?"

I Suggested That Lester "Come On By And See For Himself."

We Had A Performance Of John Steinbeck's Of Mice And Men At Our Forty-Eighth Street Theater, And Lester, His Sidemen, And The Club's Young Promoter And Booking Agent, Monte Kay, Came To Watch It One Night. For This Performance, I Took On The Role Of The Troubadour. Of Course, There Isn't A Character In Of Mice And Men Titled The Troubadour. In Order To Allow The Stagehands Time To Change Sets And To Convey The Story's Period And Location, The Director Had Conjured Up This Mysterious Character To Emerge Between Scenes And Sing Snippets Of Woody Guthrie And Leadbelly Ballads. Never In A Million Years Would I Have The Guts To Pretend To Be A Vocalist On Stage. As The Troubadour, Though, I Was Only Playing A Role While Performing My Songs. That Was The Turning Point For Me.

The Jazz Fans Remained Until The Very End And Were Quite Kind As I Escorted Them Back To The Roost For A Drink After The Show. At Least They Were Made Aware Of My Actions Now. For Me, It Was Plenty. I Had No Idea They Would Provide Such A Life-Altering Recommendation Based On My Singing.

The Workshop Parts Continued Arriving, But By The Beginning Of 1948, The Excitement I'd Had At Being Part Of Such A Fantastic Group Had Faded. It Was Meant To Help Me Break Into The Acting Industry, But So Far I Have Been Unable To Get Even A Little Role In An Off-

Broadway Production Or Sign With An Agency. They Were All Making Progress, Receiving Breaks, And Having Much To Discuss During Get-Togethers When I Saw Them. Because Of My Status As A Black Actor, I Found Myself More Isolated From My Peers. Nothing Marguerite Said Could Assuage The Rage Brought On By The Return Of The Loneliness I'd Felt So Acutely In My Childhood, The Horrible Sensation Of Not Belonging. In Our Prejudiced, All-White World, There Are So Few Roles For Black Performers That I Would Go On A Tirade About It. I Would Rant About How Terrible White Politics Were: People Of Color Were Being Murdered In The South, And Strom Thurmond, A Staunch Segregationist, Was Running For President. It Didn't Take Much To Set Me Off. While We Rode The Train Together, I Would Point Out The Several Ads For Cosmetics That Appeared Above Us. There Were A Disproportionate Number Of Black Commuters, So Why Were All The Models White?

As My Career As An Actor Dimmed, I Became More Involved In Political Activism. In Order To Mobilize The Rank And File To Fight For Improved Salaries And Working Conditions, I Helped Put On Agitprop Plays At Several Union Rooms. During The Summer Vacation, My Two Roommates And I Traveled To Pennsylvania's Beaver Lodge, A Gorgeous Union Retreat, To Assist The Entertainment Staff In Putting On A Variety Of Plays And Sing-Alongs. Memory Is Hazy, But I Do Recall Opposing Inequity And Injustice With Pete Seeger, Lee Hays, Josh White, And Others The War Had Been Fought For Democracy, But Now That It Had Been Won, It Seemed To Be Failing Us At Every Turn. The Administration Actively Prevented Strikes And Restricted Free Expression. It Considered Its Own People Who Held "Undemocratic" Opinions To Be Traitors. In The South,

Many Returning Black Veterans Had The "Uppity" Idea That They, Too, Had Fought A War For Democracy, And This Led To A Wave Of Beatings And Lynchings That The War Did Little To Halt. Isaac Woodard, A Distinguished Black Soldier From South Carolina, Was One Of The First Casualties. He And The White Greyhound Bus Driver Got Into An Altercation In February 1946. The Driver Immediately Called The Police When They Reached Their Next Stop. The Cops Hauled Him Off The Bus And Gouged Out Both Of His Eyes, Despite The Fact That He Was Covered With Medals. At Rallies He Would Speak, His Hollow Eye Sockets A Horrifying Reminder Of The Damage Prejudice Can Do. Thousands More Victims Of Brutality In The Postwar South Were Never Identified Or Brought To Justice.

Paul Robeson Performed And Gave Speeches At A Few Of The Events. He Was The Headliner, And I Was Just An Usher. But I Did Go Up To Him And Explain That I Had Read His Previous Speech And Found It Really Inspiring, As Well As That I Had Been In The Play At The Ant. He Found Me, And When He Did, He Gave Me His Famous Smile. You're Here! "Oh, Harry. Glad To Have You Back.

In Hindsight, I Saw How The Connections I Had Developed With The Other Actors In The Class Started To Suffer Under The Weight Of My Politicking. I Had A Heavy Burden Of Shame And Responsibility On My Shoulders, And I Made Other People Feel Bad About Themselves If They Didn't Care As Much About Social Concerns As I Did. Even Though I Was Liked By Them More Than I Realized, I Was Ultimately Too Much For Them. The Reality Was That Some Of My Anger Was Not Directed At The Difficulties, My Parents, Or Our Financial Situation, But Rather At The Fact That My Peers Were Starting To Gain Jobs, Including Roles In Professional

Theater Performances Outside Of School. Nothing Was Coming Through To Me.

My Good Fortune Finally Dawned Upon Me One Day During That Cold Season. Osceola Archer, The Ant Director Who Placed Me In My First Performances, Called Me. She Was Working On A Sojourner Truth Play, On The Abolitionist And Civil Rights Pioneer Who Was A Black Woman. She Suggested I Portray The Son Of Sojourner. This Was A Tremendous Deal For Me. Erwin Piscator's Works Were, Figuratively Speaking, Also Off-Broadway. However, They Were Not Commercial Competitors Since They Were Staged And Funded By A University. The 92nd Street Y Is Hardly The Palace Or The Winter Garden, But That's Where Sojourner Truth Will Have Her World Premiere. Nonetheless, Strictly Speaking, It Would Be My First Off-Broadway Show. What's More, I'd Get To Perform Beside Muriel Smith, A Rising Talent In The New York Theatrical Scene. Smith Was Well Praised For Her Fourteen-Month Run In Carmen Jones, The All-Black Broadway Adaptation Of The Bizet Opera Carmen By Oscar Hammerstein Ii. Having Already Made A Name For Herself As A Singer, She Anticipated That Her Performance As Sojourner Would Propel Her To Other Broadway Roles. Maybe I'm To Blame, At Least A Little, That It Didn't Work Out.

There Were No Hiccups On Opening Night, April 20, 1948. The Issue Occurred At The Beginning Of The Matinee The Next Day. Muriel Smith's Co-Star In The Program Was A White Lady Whose Kid Was Friends With My Character. Like Huck Finn And Tom Sawyer, The Two Of Us Were Always Getting Into Some Kind Of Scrape. The Performance Began With The Audience Being Pursued Across The Stage By Police; We Were Then Instructed To Jump Through A Basement Window And

Find Ourselves In The Midst Of A Clandestine Gathering Of Abolitionists. My Buddy Took The Plunge First. When He Did This During The Matinee, His Trousers Tore All The Way Up The Rear, Exposing His Lack Of Underwear. Even Though Several Of My Other Actors Sent Me Angry Glances Behind The Scenes, I Still Found It Comical To Watch Him Throw A Hand Back To Attempt To Conceal His White Behind. The Most Irate Of The Bunch Was Muriel Smith. It Was Her Play, Her Means Of Expression, And I Was Poking Fun At It. After Our Third And Last Performance At The 92nd Street Y, She Remained Silent For The Rest Of The Day And Throughout Our Run At The American Negro Theatre A Month Later.

There Were Two Silver Linings To That Performance In The City. One Claimed That Eleanor Roosevelt Saw It, As The Playwright, Katherine Garrison Biddle, Was A Friend Of Roosevelt's. In Her "My Day" Column That Week, Mrs. Roosevelt Referred To Muriel Smith As Having A "Beautiful Voice" And Said That She Was "A Really Fine Actress," Which Helped Assuage Some Of The Guilt I Felt. The Line, "Many Of The Men Impressed Me Also," Was The First Critical Praise I'd Seen In Paper, And I Interpreted It As Such. What's More, Marguerite Was In Attendance For The Harlem Show.

When Marguerite Saw Me Perform That May Evening, Something Snapped. She Approached Me Shortly After And Hugged Me From The Heart. We Went Down The East River Drive's Promenade After The Play, Enjoying The Glimmering Bridges Above And Below Us. I Pushed Her Toward The Railing And Threatened To Toss Her Into The Water If She Didn't Agree To Marry Me, And She Gave In. After A Few Screams, She Finally Did. On June 18th, We Agreed To Meet.

For The Following Three Weeks, I Was Anxious That Marguerite Might Have Second Thoughts. On June 18, Though, When I Picked Her Up From Bethany Day Nursery During Her Lunch Break, She Was Still Enthusiastic About Marrying A Black Actor With Limited Career Possibilities. She Had Even Found A Suitable Wedding Gown. An Aunt Of Marguerite's From Jersey City Turned There To Represent The Byrds, And Mrs. Bears, Her Supervisor And My Ally, Came Down To City Hall With Us As Witnesses. Marguerite Had Told Her Parents The News The Night Before, And They Had Shown No Sign Of Concealing Their Shock At Their Daughter's Hasty Action. Nobody In My Family Was There. And Why Should They? My Mother Was Not Happy With My Young Marriage, But She Was Unhappy About Pretty Much Anything I Did. Bill Wright, My Stepfather, And His Then-Four And Six-Year-Old Children Would Not Have Traveled Here Without Her. Since Millie Had Remarried And He Was No Longer Had To Pay Monthly Child Support, We Had No Contact, But It Wasn't Because He Disapproved Of Me. My Younger Brother Dennis Has Hatred Against Me Since I'm The One Who Isn't There And Has To Fend For Myself. There Was Never A Time When I Felt Sorry For Myself. Just The Way Things Were.

My New Wife, Marguerite, And I Took Our Honeymoon In The Same Pennsylvania Union Lodge Where My Roommates And I Had Hosted Employees Throughout The Previous Winter And Spring. Because I Committed To Working As A Paid Member Of The Entertainment Crew For The Duration Of The Summer, The Organizers Lavished Us With Lavish Treats. After 10 Wonderful Days, Marguerite Returned To Her Employment At Bethany Day Nursery In Manhattan. A Lot Of The Time

During The Following Several Months, The $75 She Made At Bethany Was The Only Thing Keeping Us From Being Completely Destitute. I Was In My Twenties. As An Actor, I Was A Black Man Whose G.I. Bill Funds Had Just Expired. Here We Have A Married Black Actor Who Can't Get Job. After The Summer Is Through, I'll Have To Start Looking For A Job And An Apartment For The Two Of Us. Since Marguerite Was Expecting A Child In August, She Would Need A Higher Paying Job Than Moving Clothing Racks In The Garment Area.

Chapter 5

That Night In January Of 1949, I Recall A Chilly Rain And A Stiff Breeze That I Attempted To Shield From With The Collar Of My Blue Peacoat. Pee Wee Marquette, The Little Guy In The Admiral's Uniform Who Waited Outside The Royal Roost And Wooed Customers With His Constant Chatter, Messed Up My Name As Usual As I Entered. That's Right, Harry Bella Buddha! Mr. Harry, How Are You Doing Today?"

I Dithered. Marguerite Was Correct; While I Was Putting Off Dealing With My New Obligations As A Spouse And Soon-To-Be Parent, I Was Wasting Away The Winter Evenings At The Roost. Although The Weather Outside Was Sub-Zero, The Roost's Cozy Confines Made It Seem Like Home. A Calm, Smooth, And Flawless Solo On The Tenor Saxophone Drew Me In As I Opened The Door. The Music Of Lester Young And His Band Was Too Good To Pass Up.

Some Rough Months Had Passed For Me. The Completion Of My G.I. I Couldn't Afford To Continue My Studies At The New School's Dramatic Workshop, So I Had To Drop Out. No Further Parts Had Come My Way After My Off-Broadway Debut In Sojourner Truth. Full-Time In The Garment District For $40 A Week, I Was Still Moving Racks Of Clothing. And I Couldn't See The Impact My Activity Was Having Right Now. Henry Wallace's Presidential Campaign Fizzled, Blacks Were Still Being Killed In The Segregated South, And The Nation Didn't Seem Any Closer To A Classless Society Despite All The Demonstrations, Agitprop Plays, And Sing-Alongs.

During Those Several Months, I Really Considered Leaving The Theater Industry. I Was Aware That Marguerite Wanted Me To Get My Life In Order By

Obtaining My Ged, Enrolling In College, And Getting A Stable Career. Her Family Was Quite Forthright In Telling Her She Was Making A Huge Mistake By Marrying Me. Both Her Family And Her Friends Had Anticipated She Would Marry A Respectable Black Graduate Student, Or At The Very Least, That New York Times Writer. Instead, She Fell For A Youngster Who Was Clever And Quick On His Feet, Who Was Entertaining To Be Around, And Who Was Both Sympathetic And Endearing To Her. I Used Her Feelings For Me As A Hook In Our Romance. I Felt More Pressure To Be A Good Father Now That She Was Expecting Our Kid. In My Head, I Could Hear My Parents Having Their Same Fights Over And Again. Why Don't You Get A Real Job, Harry?To Paraphrase, "I Do What I Can," "It's Not Enough!"You're Asking Too Much," She Said. "All I Want Is For You To Be A Good Husband And Parent.Most Importantly, I Didn't Want To Embarrass Myself In Front Of Marguerite As My Dad Had In Front Of Millie.

When Lester And His Band Finished Their Play That Night At The Roost, They Invited Me To Sit Up Front. When Asked, "How Do You Feel?"Lester Enquired. That's How He Always Phrased It. Afterwards He First Came To See My Performance As The Troubadour In Of Mice And Men, We've Been Good Friends In The Months Afterwards. I Had Informed Him About My Time Spent In Portsmouth Naval Prison For Two Weeks, And He Had Told Me About His Own Time Spent In A Prison That Was Far Worse. Lester Had Been Drafted And Was Stationed In Alabama When He Was Busted For Drug Possession. The Rap Was Upgraded To Miscegenation Once Police Discovered His Girlfriend Was White. Interracial Sexual Activity, Whether Or Not It Results In Marriage, Is Considered Miscegenation Under Alabama Law. Lester

Spent The Remainder Of The War Locked Up In A Military Jail, An Ordeal That Would Eventually Play A Role In Contributing To His Mental Breakdown.

I Informed Him, "My Feelings Aren't Doing So Well," And I Went On To Describe How Hopeless The Situation Was. Why Don't You Try To Get A Position Via Monte?One Of Lester's Associates Chimed In. There Will Be "Something To Tide You Over."

Newly Appointed Manager Of The Royal Roost, Monte Was Named Monte Kay.

"I'm Not A Singer," I Said. I Was Faking What You Saw. It So Happened That There Was Singing Involved."

Another Of The Extras Suggested, "Have A Word With Monte."

To My Surprise, Monte Didn't Need To Be Convinced; He Enjoyed The Same Performances I Had At The Theater On Forty-Eighth Street. Monte Was My Age; He Was An Olive-Skinned Sephardic Jew With A Passion For Jazz Who Believed His Job At The Roost Would Lead To Booking His Own Acts. The Mafia Controlled The Roost (As They Did Other Major Nightclubs In The Nation), But Monte Was Still Able To Hire Anybody He Wanted To Perform There. Monte Would Take A Plane To St. Louis If He Heard A Local Child Was A Talented Trumpet Player. Singing Throughout The Breaks: How About It?We Could Give It A Go For A Couple Of Weeks And See How It Works," He Proposed To Me.

"But I Don't Have A Repertoire," I Said.

"Well, You Can Sing," Monte Said. "And It's Simple To Prepare Enough Songs For A Break."

Monte Sought Out Al Haig, Lester's Pianist And The Only Non-African-American Member Of Lester Young's Band And A Frequent Collaborator Of The Likes Of Dizzy

Gillespie, Charlie Parker, And Miles Davis. And Al Replied He'd Be Pleased To Help.

Monte Reassured Me, "Don't Worry; We'll Pay You, Too—Scale. Weekly Payments Of $70."

Just Seventy Bucks! To Break Into Song!

My Roommate Alan Greene Contributed A Song Called "Lean On Me," And Al And I Polished Up A Couple Classics, Including "Pennies From Heaven," For A Dramatic Workshop Musicale At The Houston Street Theater That Week. Middleman, What Now? Is The Name Of The Revue., To Which The Students Had Contributed Songs Or Vignettes In Whatever Form They Choose, Had Centered On Troops Returning From The War And Attempting To Assimilate Into Postwar Life. The Title Track From My Album, "Recognition," Was Inspired By My Experiences As A Black Veteran In A Mostly White Country.

They Call Me A Nomad.

Going From Town To Town Aimlessly

I'm Trying To Locate A Quiet Spot.

A Place To Rest My Tired Head.

As A Final Note, I Sang, "I'm Gonna Put My Shoulder To The Wheel Of Freedom And Help It Roll Along."

I Went Out And Got A Blue Suit, Although A Used One That Still Looks Great, To Wear On My Big Night. The Fact That I'd Be Making $70 A Week Intrigued Marguerite, But Not Enough For Her To Come Hear Me Out. She Thought Singing Was Only For Fun, Whereas Acting Was A Questionable Profession.

My Stomach Was In Knots, My Hands Were Sweating, And My Mouth Was Dry During Lester's First Performance The Following Tuesday Night. I Was About To Leave When The Game Ended And Everyone Disappeared Except For Al. Before I Could Do Anything,

Pee Wee Marquette Appeared Onstage, His Admiral's Cap Tilted In A Swaggering Manner. Monte Had Snatched Him From The Street To Do The Deed. "Gentlemen, It Is With Great Pleasure That We At The Royal Roost Present Our Newest Discovery, Harry Bella Buddha!"

As I Staggered On The Stage, Al Nodded And Smiled And Added A Flourish On The Piano. Then Something Strange Occurred, An Event That Has Stuck With Me As Clearly Now As It Did Sixty Years Ago.

Tommy Potter Joined Us On Stage, Grabbed A Bass, And Began Playing. I Stared At Him In Disbelief And Perplexity. He Smiled And Nodded At Me.

Max Roach Then Slipped Out From Behind The Drum Kit.

Charlie Parker Came Out From The Wings And Started Playing The Saxophone.

Charlie Parker, Al Haig, Tommy Potter, And Max Roach.

It Seemed Unbelievable To Me. A Twenty-One-Year-Old Singer Nobody Had Ever Heard Of Was Making His Debut In A Nightclub Intermission, And Four Of The World's Best Jazz Players Had Just Volunteered To Be His Support Band. They Weren't Sitting In Because They Felt I Had A Clever Use Of Phrase Or The Finest Scat Going. They Came Out To Give This Child, Who Frequented The Club, A Proper Farewell.

Al Immediately Began Singing "Pennies From Heaven" In E Flat. But If Charlie Had Been Reminded Of The Sixteen-Bar Introduction, He Had Already Forgotten It. Charlie Blew A Riff On His Saxophone As I Was Going To Speak. My Mind Was Utterly Blown, And I Just Stood There Nodding Along, Happy And Afraid. The Introduction Was Completely Indistinguishable To Me. When Al Gave Me The Go-Ahead, I Didn't Even Think Twice About It.

The Audience At The Roost That Night Was Great, And I Received A Big Hand For "Pennies." The Clapping Became Stronger After Each Of The Following Four Songs. When I Finished, The Audience Gave Me A Standing Ovation, And When I Worked Up The Courage To Look At Monte, I Saw Him Sitting Off To The Side Grinning Like A Cheshire Cat, As If He Had Known All Along That This Would Be The Response I Would Get.

Nothing I Said That Night To Express My Gratitude To The Guys Was Enough. No Matter How Much I Tried To Make Up For Their Incredible Kindness, I Knew I Would Never Be Able To. As Soon As They Walked Out On Stage And Started Playing For Me, I Was Instantly Given Credibility By The Audience. So Everyone Stopped Talking, Stopped Waving Down Waiters For More Drinks, And Simply Listened Out Of Interest. I'd Had My Opportunity, Too. All I Could Do Was Keep An Eye Out For Chances To Aid Some Undiscovered Talent In The Future, The Way Those Men Had Helped Me, And Hope That When They Arrived, As They Did, I Was Able To Pay It Forward In A Tiny Manner.

Monte Kept Adding Weeks To My Contract Until I Had Worked For Him For A Total Of Twenty-Two Months. Two Or Three Intermissions A Night Were My Opportunity To Showcase My Growing Repertory. Now That The First Night's All-Star Sendoff Had Over, Al Haig Was My Sole Backup, But He Was More Than Enough. When I Performed In Front Of Enthusiastic Crowds, Monte Increased My Salary From $100 To $200 Each Week. The Sight Was Stunning. One Spring Evening, I Went From Being A Nobody Who Didn't Believe He Could Sing To Accepting A Plaque From The Pittsburgh Courier, An African-American Newspaper, As The Most

Promising Young Vocalist In The Nation On The Carnegie Hall Stage.

My Voice And Appearance Were Well Received By The Audience. One Gossip Writer Called Me "The Gob With A Throb," Which Means "A Complete Idiot With A Stab Wound." But I Could Have Performed The Same Songs At A Thousand Different Jazz Bars Throughout The Country And Had The Same Result. The Roost Was Not Your Typical Bar. It Was The Mecca Of Jazz And The Cradle Of Bebop In The Winter Of 1949, With Symphony Sid, The Best Jazz Dj On The Radio, Broadcasting The Nightly Onslaught Of Sizzling Licks From A Glassed-In Booth In The Rear Of The Club. Symphony Sid Was Just As Instrumental In My Success As Monte Kay.

Originally From The Lower East Side, White Hipster Symphony Sid (Born Sidney Tarnopol) Became Known As The "Dean Of Jazz" For Introducing Black Jazz Performers To Mainstream Radio Listeners. Lester Young Sang About Him On "Jumpin' With Symphony Sid" (With The Lyrics "The Dial Is All Set Right Close To Eighty...") To Promote His Regular Program On Wjz. However, He Often Did Live Broadcasts From The Roost In Conjunction With Monte. Sid Ruled From The Back Booth The First Week Of My Intermission Stint, Commanding His Supporters To Pay Attention. A Lot Of Interesting Things Are Happening Here At The Royal Roost, And We Have A Fascinating Performer In Harry Belafonte. This Is A Fantastic Tale, You Guys. He Had Been In The Garment Area With A Rack Of Garments A Week Before. At The Roost, He's Starting To Really Cram Them In! Because His Narrative Is So Similar To That Of Cinderella, We Refer To Him As "The Cinderella Gentleman.""

During That First Week, I Brought On Monte And Symphony Sid As Co-Managers And Hired Virginia Wicks,

The Roost's Publicist, To Represent Me As Well. Virginia Was The Only One I Had To Pay, For Working The Phones To Get The Jazz Reviewers In, And For Planting A Mention Here And There, But Monte And Sid Would Assist Me For Free Until I Earned Some Significant Money. Both Monte And Sid Agreed That A Record Was An Immediate Need For Me. The Guts To Make It Happen Was With Monte.

He Started Roost Records, Found A Studio, And Recruited Several Musicians Overnight. Machito And His Orchestra Were The Most Popular Latin Band In The United States. Howard Mcghee On Trumpet And Brew Moore On Tenor Saxophone Both Had Impressive Solos During The Recording Of "Lean On Me," One Of The Tracks. On The Other Side Came My Own Composition Entitled "Recognition."

Monte's Gift To Symphony Sid, A Copy Fresh Off The Press, Was Presumably Still Warm. "Listen To This, My Fellow Hipsters," Sid Crooned That Night To His Radio Listeners, "The Cinderella Gentleman, Harry Belafonte, Has Gone And Made A Record." He Avoided Jail Time By Remaining In His Glass Booth At The Roost, And Because To His Tireless Promotion, The Album Sold 10,000 Copies In The Big Apple. Monte Gushed To Me That If We Kept Up That Pace, We'd Sell A Million Books Throughout The Nation. The Only Problem Was That Nobody Else In New York Carried Roost Records But Monte And Virginia.

Paul Robeson And His Wife Eslanda Resided In Harlem's Most Exclusive Residence, Edgecombe Avenue. My Roost-Free Evening Saw Me Having Supper With The Robesons And Marguerite. Their Flat On Edgecombe Avenue Was Decorated With Images Of Robeson On Stage And Signatures From Black Leaders Throughout The Globe. This Area Is Known As Sugar Hill, And It Is The

Best Portion Of A Very Attractive Neighborhood. The Eight Or Ten Invited Guests Included John Oliver Killens, Whose Upcoming Novel Youngblood Is About A Black Family In Georgia At The Turn Of The Century, Langston Hughes, The Poet I'd Glimpsed On Harlem Streets, And None Other Than Dr. W.E.B. Du Bois, Who Laughed Indulgently When I Told Him I'd Gone To The Chicago Public Library To Look For The Great "Ibid" He'd Referenced In So Many Of His Footnotes.

Over A Big Table Illuminated By Two Enormous Silver Candelabras, The Discourse Over Dinner Was Electric With Heated Political Debate. With The Onset Of The Cold War, Robeson's Decision To Go To Paris For The World Peace Congress, Which Was Sponsored By The Soviet Union, Was Met With Widespread Criticism. After He Returned And Spoke The Words That Brought Down The Entire Might Of The Federal Government Onto His Head, I Recall Going Back To Sugar Hill For Supper, Where I Overheard Several Of His Guests Debating The Wisdom Of His Leaving.

Robeson Had Upset Many Americans When, In Paris, He Said, "It Is Unthinkable That American Negroes Would Go To War On Behalf Of Those Who Have Oppressed Us For Generations [By Which He Meant The United States] Against A Country Which In One Generation Has Raised Our People To The Full Dignity Of Mankind [By Which He Meant The Soviet Union]." But He Didn't Deny The Feeling Was There.

There Was No Discussion Of Whether Or Not To Hold Out For Civil Rights At The Banquet; Rather, Robeson And His Guests Focused On Which Ones Blacks Should Prioritize Before Returning To Fight For White America. To The Black Bourgeois, Like Marguerite's Family, President Truman's July 1983 Executive Order Officially

Desegregating The Entire U.S. Military Was A Huge Stride Forward. Robeson, In His Authoritative Position At The Head Of The Table, Downplayed Truman's Action As An Attempt To Court Black Northern Votes In The 1948 Presidential Race. It May Have Been The Deciding Factor In Truman's Win Against Wallace And Dewey, And No One Knew It. If Truman Had Been Reelected, What Would He Be Doing For Black People? As Far As Robeson Could Tell, There Was Nothing. Until The Final Colored Only Sign In The South Is Taken Down, Until The Last Segregated School Is Desegregated, And Until Every Black Person Is Permitted To Vote In Free And Fair Elections, Black People Will Not Feel Patriotic Again. We All Sat Around Robeson's Table And Agreed That Truman Was The Most Cynical Politician We'd Ever Seen, And That Only Widespread Public Pressure Would Force Him To Take Action On Racial Rights Issues.

The Truman Government Had Denounced The Civil Rights Congress, An Alliance Of Labor And Negro Organizations, As A Communist Front, And Robeson Had Been Invited To Headline A Benefit Performance For Them In Peekskill, New York, At The End Of August. A Crucifix Was Blazing On A Nearby Hill When Robeson And His Guests Drove Up To The Rally Location And Saw Locals Assaulting Early Attendees With Baseball Bats. When Robeson Wanted To Get Out Of The Vehicle And Face The Throng, His Hosts Held Him Back. The Show Was Postponed Till Later In The Week. I Was Among The 20,000 Individuals Who Showed Out To See Robeson, Pete Seeger, And Woody Guthrie Play This Time. The Audience Was Protected From The Irate Locals Thanks To The Trade Unions' Well-Organized Security Perimeter. On Their Way Out, Concertgoers, However, Were Met By A Mile-Long Line Of Counterprotesters Chanting, "Go

Back To Russia, You Niggers," And Pouring Just As Much Hate At The "White Niggers" Who Had Paid To Attend The Concert. Police Officers Watched As Concertgoers Were Dragged From Their Vehicles And Abused. Because Of My Anonymity, I Didn't Have To Worry About The Implications Of Attending That Peekskill Rally, But Robeson Was Soon Compelled To Give Up His Passport Under The Mccarran Act And Was Harassed By The Fbi For The Rest Of The 1950s.

Everyone Who Attended Those Sugar Hill Meals Was A Socialist, At Least In The Nebulous Sense Of Demanding Racial And Economic Equality In The United States. Except For Marguerite, Who Remained Silent Since She Knew Her Opinions Would Shock The Others. She Came With Me To The First Two Meals, But Then She Stopped Coming. When Invites Arrived, She'd Give Me An Arched Look And Encourage Me To Have Fun As If I Were Going To A Poker Night With The Guys.

Marguerite Was Still Residing In The Dormitory At The Bethany Day Nursery, And As A Loyal Supporter, Mrs. Bears Allowed Me To Remain There As Well. But With Marguerite's Expanding Tummy, It Was Evident That Plans Would Have To Be Altered. Marguerite Traveled Down To Washington With Her Family Early That Spring So That She Might Give Birth At The Same Segregated Black Hospital Where Her Mother Had Given Birth To Her. Adams Private Hospital. I Started An Exhaustive Search For The Ideal Home For Our Family Of Three In The Harlem Area. I Was Looking For An Affordable Home With A Park Or River View And At Least Four Bedrooms. I Was Never Able To Locate The Dwelling. I Had Moved Into A Fourth-Floor Walk-Up At 501 West 156th Street By The Time My Daughter Adrienne Michelle Was Born On May 27, 1949. Despite My Mother's Constant

Complaining, I Thought We Might Forge A New Bond Now That I Was Married With A Place Of My Own And A Glimmer Of A Career. The Apartment Had Three Rooms Instead Of Four, But The Rent Was Reasonable At Fifty-Five Dollars A Month. Without Marguerite's Reliable $75 Weekly Income, I Never Would Have Dared To Sign A Lease For An Apartment Given My Newfound Insecurity As A Nightclub Singer. I Used The Daylight Hours To Finish Arranging The Furniture And Cleaning The House In Preparation For Marguerite's Return In June. She Brought Her Mother, Who Glared Over Adrienne Michelle In Protectiveness, To Move Home With Us And Work As A Full-Time Nanny. I Addressed Her As Mrs. Byrd, And It Never Occurred To Either Of Us To Use Her First Name Instead. The In-Laws Were In Good Hands With Mimi.

I Didn't Really Like Having Mimi Around The Place, But I Understood Why She Was There. By The Time Adrienne Was Born, I Was A Part-Time Parent At Best, Having Moved On From The Roost To A Variety Of Out-Of-Town Clubs Including Chicago's Black Orchid And Philadelphia's Rendez-Vous Room.

My Hands Were Crossed Over My Stomach Like I Had A Stomachache As I Stood Rigidly In The Limelight In My New Suit And Pencil Mustache. The Number Of Songs I Could Play Had Increased, Albeit I Was Leaning More Toward Pop Than Jazz At Monte And Virginia's Urging. My New Employers Saw That I Was Attracting More Ladies Than Males, So They Had Me Sing Songs Meant To Make Them Feel All Warm And Fuzzy Inside. After Performing Such Oldies As "Skylark," "Lover," "Stardust," And "The Nearness Of You," I Remained Up Drinking With The Musicians And Trying To Figure Out How My One-Time Stint At The Roost, Which Was Supposed To

Be A Stopgap Until I Got Acting Work, Had Morphed Into A Full-Time Career.

It Made Me Feel Like A Phony. I Had Never Taken Voice Lessons Before. Miss Shepherd's Piano Lessons Had Not Prepared Me Even To Read Music. Monte And Virginia Continued Telling Me I Had Natural Talent, But I Knew I Couldn't Compete With The Likes Of Billy Eckstine, Nat King Cole, Or Frank Sinatra When It Came To Singing Standards. It Was All There On The Packaging. My First Major Recording Session, The First Of Two For Capitol Records That Monte Negotiated For Me, Took Place On July 19, 1949. Both Of The 78 Rpm Singles I Released Included Covers Of Famous Tin Pan Alley Ballads, With The First Being "How Green Was My Valley" And "Deep As The River" And The Second Featuring "They Didn't Believe In Me" And "Close Your Eyes," But Sales Were Dismal. I Recorded Four Additional Songs On December 20, 1949, But None Of Them Were Huge Hits: "Farewell To Arms," "Whispering," "I Still Get A Thrill," And "Sometimes I Feel Like A Motherless Child."

The Roost Had Already Closed At That Time Because Its Owners Had Been Unable To Negotiate A New Lease With The Building's Landlord. The Celebration, However, Had Just Relocated A Few Streets North To A New Location On Broadway, Close To 52nd Street. The Legendary Jazz Club Is Now Known As Birdland In Honor Of Charlie Parker, But The Outstanding Musicians And Helpful Staff Have Remained The Same. Lester Young Performed A Tune He Called "Birdland" On The First Night Of The Club's Existence. In Addition To Being On The Inaugural Bill, Charlie Was Instrumental In The Establishment Of The Venue, And Monte Kay Was Hired As The Manager. Monte Had Me Perform At Bop City, A New Club Across The Street From Where Birdland Had

Just Debuted. There I Was Performing In A "History Of Jazz" Performance, Where My Quintet And I Performed Standards From Dixieland Through Bebop. The Other Singers Were Great (Among Them Was Brock Peters, Who Played The Black Man Accused Of Rape In The Film Adaptation Of To Kill A Mockingbird), But I Couldn't Help But Feel Like An Imposter—Less A Singer Than An Actor Pretending To Be One.

Erwin Piscator And His Dramatic Workshop Left An Impression On Me That I Couldn't And Didn't Want To Get Rid Of. I Had Dove Headfirst Into The Realm Of Rigorous Academic Study, Devoured The Works Of Shakespeare And Aristophanes, Ibsen And Sartre, And Soaked In Piscator's Devotion To The Theater As A High Art And Important Social Duty. Suddenly, I Was Living A New Life Where I Sang Ridiculous Songs. In The Calm Of The Baccalatta's Night, Would You Adore Me?I Understood That Most Vocalists Didn't Pay Attention To The Words, But That Was Never An Issue For Me. When I Sang Those Lyrics, I Felt So... Fake. I'd Gone Too Far And Made A Mistake. Unfortunately, I Had Strayed Far From My Normal Territory.

In Between My Club Engagements, I Would Search For Acting Opportunities And Go On Auditions. There Were No Opportunities For Black Actors (Apart From Butlers And Manservants), But I Saw Potential In Casting White Actors As Black. I Remember Arguing With White Casting Directors Over The Possibility Of Having A Black Actor Play The Companion Of A White Female Lead.I Tried Again And Over Again Without Success, But With My Newfound Financial Freedom, I Enrolled In Further Dramatic Workshop Classes Whenever I Could. I Was Able To Play A Black Character In A Production Of Robert Sherwood's The Petrified Forest Because I Aggressively

Pursued The Position. To My Surprise, Not Even Piscator Considered Me For Any White Roles.

Ironically, Whenever I Performed A New York Bar, My White Dramatic Workshop Friends Would Show Out To Hear Me And Gush Over My Amazing Success In Between Sets. Hollywood Stars Like Tony Curtis, Walter Matthau, Marlon Brando, And Rod Steiger Would Attend. They Saw Me As The Man Who Was Already On His Path To Greatness Because Of His Stable Job. Henry Fonda, Who First Saw Me Play At The Roost, Quickly Became One Of My Most Devoted New Admirers. He Was A Huge Jazz Fan And, Later On, A Staunch Civil Rights Advocate Who Always Responded To My Pleas For Assistance.

In Addition To The Acclaim, These Club Appearances Also Provided Me With Some Much-Needed Sustenance. I Had Worked My Way Up From Janitorial Assistant To Making Almost $350 Per Week By The Time I Performed For Several Weeks At New York's Café Society In The Spring Of 1950. I Simply Had To Pay Taxes And Virginia For Feeding Material To The Press Since Monte And Sid Were Generous Enough To Forego Any Commission, Telling Me They'd Start Collecting Cuts When I Performed The Copacabana. I Was Able To Assist Marguerite And Adrienne With Their Financial Needs. For The First Time In My Life, I Had Enough Savings To Propose To Monte That Maybe I Might Take A Long Hiatus From Singing To Give Acting A Go. After All, I Had Just Cut Three Additional Singles For Jubilee Records, And They Weren't Doing Any Better Than My Capitol Efforts. Isn't It Time To Confront Facts?

Then Monte Would Moan And Give Me Another Dose Of His Motivational Speech. See How Far You've Come, He'd Encourage. You're Playing Bigger Clubs Every

Season. This Is The Foundation, He'd Explain. Each One Is Superior Than The Previous. This Is The Proper Strategy For Winning. If You Want To Succeed, You Have To Get In The Game.

In The Late Autumn Of 1950, Monte Contacted Me With Some Very Exciting News. Now That I Had Landed A Two-Week Engagement At Miami's Martha Raye's Five O'clock Club, Paying $500 Per Week, The Next Piece Of The Puzzle Was In Place. Definitely A Step In The Right Direction! However, I Warned Monte That This Would Be My First Time Traveling To The Very Segregated South. "Oh, Come On," He Answered. Yes, That's Miami!" Jewish Homeland! "You'll Be Just Fine.

I Have Performed As Far West As Chicago But Never Farther South Than Pittsburgh In My Almost Two Years As A Jazz/Pop Vocalist. I Had Felt Prejudice Practically Wherever I Went, But It Was Never Overt. Even If There Were Empty Tables Near The Restaurant's Kitchen Exit, The Maître D' Would Always Nod And Lead Me Back To The Same Table. When I Checked In, The Front Desk Agent Would Be Taken Aback And Fumble With His Reservation Book, And Once Again, I Would Be Sent To A Room On The Hotel's Top Floor That Was Originally Reserved For Maids. But When I Stepped Off The Aircraft In Miami, It Felt Like I Was Back In Elementary School.

The Five O'clock Club On Twentieth And Collins Was Named After The Notoriously Crass Comedienne Martha Raye. Its Strategy Of Providing Free Beverages At 5 O'clock Contributed At Least As Much To Its Popularity As The 24-Hour Bookmakers In The Basement. The Manager Was Really Kind And Gave Me Many Passes And Explained The Procedure When I Arrived. On The Ghetto Side Of Town, At A Relatively Inexpensive Hotel, I Would Be Spending The Night. Since White Cabbies

Wouldn't Pick Me Up And It Was Illegal For People Of Color To Hail Cabs, I Needed A Pass So That The Black Cabbie Could Take Me There. My Driver Might Have Taken Me Home As A Third Option. The Management Of The Five O'clock Club Kindly Informed That I Would Need A Permit To Play There, As Well As At Any White Cabaret, And A Third Pass To Travel After Curfew (Really A Police Card).

A Black Commercial Sector Along Avenue G In Miami's "Harlem Of The South" Sold Sweet-Potato Pies, Barbecued Chicken And Ribs, And Hot Fish Sandwiches. Black Singers Such As Billie Holiday And Bessie Smith Performed Nightly At Clubs Such As Harlem Square And Rockland Palace, Where Zoot-Suited Dandies And Their Dates, In Expensive Silk Costumes, Promenaded. Nothing About Colored Town Appealed To Me Since The Pain Of Discrimination Was So Palpable Here. I Unloaded My Belongings In The Cramped Room Provided, Wondering How On Earth I Was Going To Survive The Next Week, Much Alone The Next Two.

That Night, I Returned To The Five O'clock Club With My Passes In Hand (The Driver Had Informed Me That Curfew Was At Nine O'clock, Though Of Course Only Colored Residents Were Required To Respect It) And Vowed Not To Let My Tumultuous Emotions Show Onstage. The Audience, Composed Mostly Of White Women, Clapped Enthusiastically, And Some Patrons At The Front Tables Winked At Me. I Had Control Over Them So Long As I Was Singing Love Songs On Stage. But As The Sun Came Up, I Was Just Another Black Guy On The Run, Trying To Get Back To Colored Town Before The Authorities Caught Up With Me. And Heaven Forbid I Should Strike Up A Conversation With Any Of My New

White Female Followers As We Walk Out Of The Club. This Might Lead To Serious Legal Consequences.

The Manager Came Back To Inform Me That He Wanted Me For Another Week After I Had Performed Well For Two Or Three Nights. In Response, I Politely Declined His Offer.

He Stared At Me In Complete Disbelief. What Are You Talking About, Harry? You May Expect To Make $500 Per Week With This Job. So The Money Isn't Good Enough For You? A Another Fifty, Perhaps? Sure, Anything.

My Head Trembled. To Which She Said, "Nope," On My Watch. When He Asked Why I Was Leaving The Segregated South, I Answered Him, "It's Not The Money."

Later That Night In My Colored Town Apartment, I Decided I'd Had Enough Of The Entire Thing, Of Being A Lounge Lizard For Lonely Ladies And Of Singing Sappy Songs I Didn't Believe In. The Next Day, I Phoned Monte To Break The News That My Time As A Pop Singer Was Over. There Will Be No Further June Moonsongs And Club Dates. After Nearly Two Years After That Fateful Night At The Roost, I Realized That Despite Monte's Best Efforts, I Had Made The Incorrect Choice And Was Now Facing The Consequences. There Was Still Time For Me To Return To New York And Give Acting My Whole Attention. Even If I Didn't Make It Big, I Would Still Follow Paul Robeson's Lead And Focus On The Things That Really Important, Both On And Offstage.

Chapter 6

The Day Of David's Wedding In New York City In The Autumn Of 2000, I Glanced Around The Room And Was Struck By How Contentedly Married Each Of My Children Seemed To Be. However Complicated Our Feelings May Have Been, We Were Nonetheless A Fortunate Family. Until I Finally Looked Over And Saw Julie. Then I Was Reminded That We Were The Odd Pair Out Among The Many That Made Up Our Extended Family.

I Was A Difficult Roommate. My Temper Would Frequently Boil Over, And My Fragile Ego Would Often Cause Me To Act In Ways I Later Came To Regret. Long After It Was Appropriate, I Continued To Dwell On Previous Hurts. When Conflicts Emerged, I Tended To Travel Even More, Which Exacerbated The Situation. Julie Would Probably Come With Me If I Gave A Performance In Paris Or London, Enjoying The Luxurious Accommodations And Attentive Service. If She Could Help It, She Would Never Visit Atlanta Or Wichita. After Realizing This, I Started Making More Frequent Trips To Less Conventional Performance Spaces Until I Was Performing At More Unusual Settings Than My Popularity Would Allow.

Although Our Public Farce May Have Been Genuine Over The Course Of Many Years, Behind The Closed Doors Of Our Enormous West End Avenue Apartment—Now That The Kids Had Grown Up And Moved Out—We Fought Tooth And Nail To Maintain Civility. The First Drink Of The Night Always Begins With The Sound Of Ice Being Poured Into Julie's Glass. I Would Drink Whenever She Did. The Toasting Was The Highlight Of The Ceremony For Me, And After That I Lost Interest. My Continued Involvement In The Drinking Game During Our Latter

Years Of Marriage Disqualified Me From Making Complaints About The State Of Our Marriage. Instead Of Encouraging Julie To Cut Down On Her Drinking, I Enabled Her. Every Night I Would Watch As The Haze Of Intoxication Engulfed Us, And I Despised Every Minute Of It. I Didn't Know How Else To Spend A Night At Home If There Was One. We Would Get Into An Argument And Then Go Off To Our Respective Wings, Frustrated And Confused. As We Continued To Carry Out These Roles, I Sought Solace In A Variety Of Diversions, Including Gambling, Sympathetic Women, And As Many Social Causes And Concerts As I Could Stomach. After A While, I Lost Track Of My Goals Since The Pursuit Of Them Had Worn Me Out. A Lady I'd Met Years Ago, Not As A Date Or A Dalliance But As A Fellow Activist With Common Acquaintances, Suddenly Gave Me A Warm, Sympathetic Feeling.

When My Friend Diahann Carroll Stood In For Elizabeth Ashley In Agnes Of God For A Week While Ashley Was On Vacation, I Met Pamela Frank For The First Time. It Was A Spectacular Night That I Will Never Forget. (Diahann's Run In The Play Began The Next Spring After That Week.) Michael Lindsay-Hogg, The Play's Director, Was Also There, As Was His Extremely Gorgeous Date. The Group Then Congregated At Sardi's For Dinner. I Found Out That Michael Went On A Date With A Photographer; She Was A Divorcee With Two Kids And Was Involved In A Number Of Human Rights Initiatives. In 1982, I Estimated That Pam Was In Her Late Thirties, Which Was A Significant Age Difference From My. Since She Already Had A Boyfriend And I Was Already Married, I Just Thought Of Her As A Really Pretty Dinner Guest. However, The Tale She Told Me That Evening Left Quite An Effect.

We've Met Previously," Pam Said. When I Was In School. When A Stunning Lady Says Anything Like That, A Guy With My Track Record Listens Up. I Moved In Closer To Her So That The Scope Of This Public Confession Would Be Limited To My Ear Canal.

"Really?"

Pam Said That She And Her Pals Had Spent Their Spring Break In The Bahamas While She Was A Student At Syracuse University. (I Learned Later That Her Best Friend, Neilia Hunter, Met And Eventually Married Joe Biden, One Of The Young Men She Met On That Trip. Pam Was Never Able To Get Over The Fact That Neilia Was Killed In A Car Accident Six Years After They First Met, Just As Biden's Political Career Was Taking Off. Pam Went On To Say That The Ladies Had Met Actor Sean Connery, Who Was Playing James Bond In The Upcoming Thunderball Film. To Remain And Act As Extras, Connery Had Asked Them To Stay. Neilia Had Hoped To Return To School Before Classes Began, But Pam And The Other Girls Had Lingered Behind To Appear In The Movie. Pam Was Standing In Line Behind Me When She Arrived At The Little Nassau Airport For Her Journey Home. (I Was On My Way To The Bahamas To Spend The Week With Sidney On One Of The Outlying Islands.) She Wanted To Snap A Photo Of Me With Her Little Minox, One Of The Trendy Newfangled Spy Cameras. I Agreed After We Had A Little Discussion.

"So, That's... It?" I Proposed To Her At Sardi's.

She Smiled Devilishly At Me. "No."

What Did I Say? "Oh," This Piqued My Interest In Her Much. As In, "Then What?"

Pam Went On To Say That Some Time Later, Her Father Had Phoned To Tell Her That A Flood Had Destroyed The Family's Garage, Along With The Several Boxes

Containing The Negatives From Pam's Photographs. Professional Photography Was Already Pam's Jam At That Point. She Was A Veteran Photographer Who Had Worked On Broadway, For Record Labels, Publishing Houses, And Political Campaigns. On Madison Avenue, She Also Had Her Own Studio Where She Photographed Families And Children. She Had Hundreds Of Negatives Stored In Those Crates, But Just A Few Were Still Usable.

"And ...?" Yes, I Did Inquire.

I Quote: "Those Were The Pictures Of You."

That's The Full Shebang.

A Powerful South African Production Called Asinamali! Arrived At Lincoln Center Four Years After The Supper At Sardi's. The Official Photographer For The Performance Was Pam, Who Had Recently Gotten Actively Involved In The Anti-Apartheid Movement And Shot Many Images To Bring Attention To The Situation In South Africa. She Was So Taken With The Performance That She Invited Me And Many Others To Check It Out In The Hopes Of Finding Financial Support. Along With Miriam Makeba, Paul Simon, And Others, I Ended Up Underwriting Its Transfer To Broadway. My Focus Shifted To Her More Often. I Began Contacting Her To Have Her Shoot Photographs At "Free South Africa" Events. It Served To Keep Us In Contact. Bob And Kathryn Altman Hosted Screening Parties For Several Of Bob's Films, And Both Pam And I Went. The More Time I Spent With Her, The More Comfortable I Felt In Her Presence. The More I Told Her How I Really Felt, The Less Pain I Was In. I Brought Her To The Carlyle For Lunch One Day. That Led To More Lunches, Which Led To Supper, Which Led To Overnight Snacks, Which Led To Morning.

There Were A Number Of Signs Of My Own Mortality Around That Time, And I Began To Really Question My

Decision To Stay Married. I Was 69 When I Found Out I Had Prostate Cancer. Like Most Guys Who Have It These Days, I Had A Procedure That Effectively Removed It, But Not Before Causing Me A Great Deal Of Physical And Emotional Distress. That It Turns Out, Sidney Had The Same Condition That I Did And Underwent Surgery A Few Weeks Before I Did. The Constant Comparisons Between Our Situations Had Reached A Farcical Level. At Least He Made It Through The Surgery, I Told Myself As I Prepared For Mine. (As I Learned More About Prostate Cancer, I Was Shocked To Hear That Black Males Were Disproportionately Likely To Be Diagnosed With The Condition. Rectal Tests Have Negative Connotations In Black Culture And Are Thus Avoided By Black Males Who Are Already Fighting Homophobia. Homophobia Probably Isn't The Only Factor, But It Does Increase The Chances Significantly. After I Got Better, I Became An Activist For The American Cancer Society, And For A While, Photos Of Shari And Me Taken By Francesco Scavullo Were Plastered All Over New York City's Subways And Buses With The Message That Black Men Should Not Be Afraid To Get Regular Rectal Exams To Check For Prostate Cancer. However, I Wondered How Much Time I Really Had Left And How I Was Using It. During My Meetings With Peter Neubauer, I Expressed My Ongoing Feeling Of Being Chased By Something I Couldn't Outrun Quickly Enough.

In 2004, I Had Finished Doing Errands In Preparation For Yet Another Road Trip And Returned To My Apartment For The Night. When I Came Home At 7, Julie Had Already Started Cooking Supper. I Could See That The Drinks Had Been Flowing Freely Since Julie Was Irritable And Had Bloodshot Eyes. Hate Me For Being Half An Hour Late? I Was Curious. Looking Back At Only The Last

Several Years, Or At Our Whole Time Together? She Then Said, "If You Decide To Ever Eat Tonight, Your Dinner's In The Oven," After Saying Some Harsh Remarks About My Tardiness. So, I'm Off To Bed.

I Was Late For Dinner, But It Wasn't The First Time. Why, Therefore, Did This Same Scenario, Which Had Been Played Out Many Times Before, Keep Coming Back To The Fore? There Was Clearly A Distinction.

To Be Honest, I'd Always Felt Frustrated And Hemmed In. I Was Trapped By My Mother, By Poverty, By Having To Take Care Of My Younger Brother When I Was Five, By My Father And What He Did, By Growing Up On A Plantation In Jamaica, By My Family's Constant Upheaval, By My Dropping Out Of School And Having To Take Menial Jobs, By Always Feeling Like A Failure And Never Trusting My Successes. I Was Also Caught By The Right-Wing Politics Of Ignorance That Only Served To Worsen The Lives Of The World's Poor. I Was Already Well Into My 70s. Perhaps I Would Always Feel Trapped By It All. Nonetheless, I Didn't Want To Waste Energy Struggling To Breathe In An Oxygen-Depleted Marriage.

"It's Over," I Said To Julie.

She Questioned, "What's Over?"

It's Over For Us As A Couple.

It Was A Sneer On Her Part. "Again?"

That Caught Me Off Guard. She Was True; I Had Taken A Few Steps Away In Anger Before, But I'd Never Gone For Good, What With Guilt And The Other Ties Of Fatherhood Keeping Me In Place. It Seemed Different This Time. It's Possible That At My Age Of Seventy-Seven, Nearly No Men Would Ever Consider Abandoning Their Wives. In Any Case, This Was The Last Straw. I Was Obligated To Take This Action. Even Though Julie Was Unaware Of It At The Time, She Probably Felt It. The End

Has Come For Us. I Was Prepared To Face Whatever Challenges A Divorce Could Bring.

For Many Years, Julie And I Had Lived Mostly Alone In Our Massive U-Shaped Apartment. We Proceeded Into The Adjoining Living Area And Closed Its Folding Doors. Since Each Half Was Initially Its Own Apartment Building, We Had No Need To Interact. The Necessary Calls To Attorneys And Financial Advisors Were Made. They Informed Me That It Would Be Very Expensive To End A 47-Year Marriage. As They Began To Outline The Steps, It Became Clear That Selling Our Flat Would Be The First Major Blow To Our Psyche.

It Was Tough To Do It. For Both Julie And I, Those Twenty-One Rooms Still Carried The Sounds Of Our Children Playing, Parties, And Weddings, And The Voices Of A Period, Including Those Of John F. Kennedy, Martin Luther King, Jr., Sidney Hillman, And The Student Nonviolent Coordinating Committee And The Black Panther Party. Martin's Attorney, Clarence Jones, Had Proclaimed Only Partially In Jest That The Flat Should Be Classified As A Historic Landmark, So That Visitors Might See Where He And His Kitchen Cabinet Had Convened So Often To Plot The Future Steps Of The Movement.

The Condo Was Put Up For Sale In August 2005, And Walt's Niece Abigail Disney Eventually Purchased It. On St. Maarten, We Also Had A House With A Breathtaking Ocean View. Chris Blackwell, A Buddy Of Mine, Sold It To Me. My Feelings About The Location Were Entirely Positive. But We Hadn't Taken The Kids Or Our Friends There Very Often Since Booze Had Transformed Many A Beautiful Sunset Into A Hazy Horizon Of Disillusionment. I Always Saw Myself There After Retirement. However, Fate Had Other Plans. Also, It Was Placed Up For Auction.

The Upper West Side Of Manhattan Was Always Going To Be My Home. I Felt Just As Much A Part Of The Community As I Did In My Flat, With Its Mix Of Students, Retirees, Performers, And Eccentrics, And Its Bustling Markets And Jewish Delicatessens, Chinese-Cuban Restaurants, And Italian Eateries. Pam And I Discovered A Beautifully Refurbished Apartment In A Big Old Building That Was Just A Few Blocks Away From The House Where I Had Spent The Previous Fifty Years Of My Life. Our New Home Was Simple, But Filled With Delight, Just Right For The Tempo Of Our Lives Now. Julie Also Relocated Close By, So Now We Both Call This Area Home. Recently, I've Been Seeing Her Out With Her Dog On Broadway, And On Occasion, We've Even Stopped To Speak. The Court Battle Is Over, And Now We Can Talk About Our Grandkids.

Even After My Divorce, I Was Still Better Off Than The Vast Majority Of The World's Population. But There Isn't An Idle Town Car In Front Of My House. I've Recently Taken An Interest In New York City's Buses And Subways Again, Where I Can Observe People Of All Different Ages, Sizes, And Skin Tones. Young Wall Street Employees, Weary Secretaries With Ipods, Joyous Youngsters From Public And Private Schools, And The Young And Elderly Swaying Together; The Classes Appear More Mixed Than When I Last Rode Those Creaking Vehicles With Any Daily Regularity. There Are Moments When I Mentally Add Up All The Donations I've Made To The Movement And Other Causes. Imagine If I Suddenly Had Everything I've Ever Wanted. Perhaps More Gratifying To The Senses... But Not Superior. In The End, What Solace Do We Have Or Even Need? Certainly Not Obscene Amounts Of Money That Choke Off Our Compassion For The Poor And The Needy.

Even Though I Was Slowing Down In My Late Seventies, I Still Became Involved In Politics When The Proper Cause Called To Me. And In My Support Of Causes, I Never Stopped Being A Proud Leftist. I Still Found Myself Admiring Virtuous Left-Wing Politicians, Or At Least Those Who Looked To Represent Socialism's Highest Principles. To No One's Surprise, I Led A Group To Meet With Hugo Chávez, The Fiery Socialist President Of Venezuela, In Early 2006. I Had The Impression That Chávez Was More Nuanced And Interesting Than The Arrogant Bully He Was Represented As In The New York Times And Other Western Media. Chávez Has Volunteered His Assistance With Disaster Relief Efforts The Summer After Hurricane Katrina. Venezuela Had Had More Than Its Fair Share Of Catastrophic Disasters, And The Country Had Therefore Gained Some Wisdom. However, President Bush Had Essentially Given Chávez The Finger, Which Was A Very Unstatesmanlike Move On His Part. After Bush Rebuffed Calls For Assistance From New Englanders As Oil Prices Skyrocketed, Chávez Said That He Would Make Venezuelan Heating Oil Accessible At Reduced Costs To Those In Need This Next Winter. (Bobby's Eldest Son Joseph Patrick Kennedy Ii, Who Now Leads A Local Nonprofit Organization Called Citizens Energy, Had Stepped In And Accepted The Offer.)

I Was Aware Of The Controversy Around Chávez. In Contrast To Bush's America, However, He Had Successfully Reduced The Unemployment Rate In His Nation By Half Since Assuming Office In 1999. As A Result Of This, Chávez Had Far More Support In Venezuela Than Bush Did In The United States. Like Every Other Left-Wing Leader Who Has Been A Target Of

U.S. Foreign Policy, I Was Curious To Hear His Side Of The Story. I Also Proposed Something To Him.

The U.S. Administration Has Been Working Hard To Destroy Coca Crops In Venezuela To Halt The Northward Flow Of Cocaine While Also Denouncing Chávez. Chávez Has Previously Questioned Why The United States Didn't Invest In Teaching Venezuelan Farmers How To Grow A Different Cash Crop. The Thought Intrigued Me. I Began To Consider Which Alternative Crop Would Be Most Beneficial For Both Venezuela And The United States To Harvest And Trade. I Traveled To Epes, Alabama, To Meet With Ralph Paige And Other Federation Of Southern Cooperatives Executives, Who Represent The Thousands Of Black Farmers In The Deep South Who Had Previously Asked For My Assistance. Coffee Was The Natural Choice According To My Epes Buddies. The South American Coffee Market Was Controlled By Brazil And Colombia For A Number Of Reasons. What If We Set Up A New Distribution Network In The United States For Venezuelan Coffee To Help It Grow There? And What If Some Of America's Fiercest But Economically Disadvantaged Citizens—Former Members Of The Bloods And The Crips And Other Inner-City Youth Groups—Could Set Up And Control That U.S. Network?

I Had Been Convinced Of The City's Potential By Father Greg Boyle, A Famed White Irish Catholic Priest Who Has Worked With L.A.'S Gangs For Decades. In Downtown Los Angeles, He Established The Homeboy Bakery, The Homeboy Café, And A Retail Shop Selling Homeboy Silkscreens. Homeboy. I Thought It Was A Great Name. Why Not Start In Los Angeles And Expand To The Rest Of The Citgo Gas Station Network, Which Is Partially Controlled By The Venezuelan Government? Homeboy Coffee Would Be A Perfect Fit For These Locations,

Whether Served Hot Or Freshly Ground. And Then Spreading Over The Whole Nation?

I Never Considered A Career As A Commodities Trader Or A Diplomatic Wheeler-Dealer. As An Activist And An Artist, Though, My Rolodex Included People From All Walks Of Life Including, Truth Be Told, Many Former Presidents. I Was Aware That An Outside Party Might Occasionally Intervene When Two Sovereign Governments Refuse To Communicate And Human Rights Problems Are Overlooked As A Consequence. That Was My Only Goal In Coming. So, I Contacted Chávez Through Intermediaries And Received An Invitation To Meet With Him.

Actor Danny Glover, Talk Show Presenter Tavis Smiley, Academic Cornel West, Ex-Gang Leader Bo Taylor, And Barrios Unidos Member Nane Alejándrez Were Among The Members Of The Delegation I Led In January 2006. We Were A Diverse Bunch, So Nobody Missed Out On The Action Because They Couldn't See Or Hear It.

We Had Been Instructed To Wait In A Huge, Fairly Nice Conference Room, When The President Eventually Came Barreling Out. When Chávez Met Our Group Of Fifteen, I Was Struck By The Individual Attention He Showed Everyone Of Us. His Was Not Only An Act For Show. That Was The Point. I Could Feel That He Was Like A Spring: Full Of Energy And Eager To Take On Whatever Challenge We Threw At Him. On The Other Hand, He Was A Ray Of Sunshine And Intense Curiosity. He Directed His Ministers, Secretaries, Academics, And Policymakers To The Other Side Of The Huge Oval Table From Us. Chávez Personally Sat In The Seat Right Beside Mine.

Chávez, Always Accompanied By A Translator, Would Sometimes Stop What He Was Saying To Consult One Of

The Volumes On The Table. Like Fidel, He Had An Opinion On Everything And Was Willing To Passionately Defend It. He Obviously Knew A Lot About The History Of Latin America And The Legal Differences Between Venezuela And Its Neighbors.

All Day Was Spent In That Meeting. For Nine Whole Hours It Continued. Chávez Saw The Whole Thing. He Seemed Really Enthusiastic About Our Coffee Plan And Often Went To His Coworkers To Ask For Help With Various Details. Everything Was Caught On Video. We Had Brought Our Own Film Team, And There Was Also One From A Venezuelan Television Network. After This All-Day Meeting, The President Took Us On A Trip On Sunday, When He Met With A Group Of Spellbound Farmers In The Rural Interior. Farmers, Women, Intellectuals, Local Leaders, Students, Athletes, And Artists All Performed Live For The President Of Venezuela On National Television As The Country Watched. Chávez Wanted Me To Address The Thousands Of Venezuelans Assembled In Front Of Us And The Millions More Watching On Television In A Completely Unscripted Moment. I Understood That This Was A Chance I Needed To Take Seriously. For The Foreign Press, I Wanted To Be Brief And Readily Translated. The Majority Of My Comments Came Straight From My Innermost Thoughts And Feelings.

Saying, "We're Here To Tell You That Not Hundreds, Not Thousands, But Millions Of The American People Support Your Revolution," I Emphasized The Widespread Support For The Uprising. While Urging The People Of Venezuela To Stay The Path And Grab Their Opportunity To Construct A Truly Egalitarian Society, I Referred To President Bush As "The Greatest Tyrant, The Greatest Terrorist In The World."

The Enthusiasm With Which Chávez Supported Our Coffee Venture Was Incredibly Motivating To Our Crew. In Light Of Our Experience Abroad, We Returned Home And Meticulously Laid Out Our Plans. Delegations From Our Organization Traveled To Caracas, Venezuela, And Delegations From Venezuela Visited California In The Following Weeks. The Next Generation Of Leaders From Both Sides Discussed Topics Of Mutual Interest. In Our Search For More Compassionate Methods Of Rehabilitation, We Even Exchanged Visits To Each Other's Jail Systems. Then, All Of A Sudden, Our New Venezuelan Coworkers Became Silent. No One Responded Our Calls, The Due Date Passed, And Work On The Project Ground To A Standstill. The Newspapers Said That Venezuela's Economy Had Entered A Tailspin. But It Seems Like A Silly Reason To Abandon A Project That May Aid Struggling Farmers.

To The Best Of My Knowledge, We Had Been Exploited. It Seems That The Hours Of Chávez's Effort Spent Facilitating A Meeting Between The Prestigious American Delegation And Venezuela's President Were Well Worth It To The Venezuelan People. There Is No Question In My Mind That The U.S. The Bush Administration Was Not Likely To Look Well On A Corporate Connection Between A Left-Wing American Musician And The Socialist Government Of Venezuela, So The State Department May Have Done Its Bit To Kill The Proposal.

I've Spent The Better Part Of The Last Half Century Helping Developing Nations And Have Come To The Conclusion That Private Persons Acting Via Back Channels For Public Benefit May Accomplish A Great Deal. However, Projects With White Wall Street

Volunteers Are More Likely To Succeed Than Those With Black Volunteers From The Middle Class.

Truly, I Believed—And Continue To Believe—That George W. Bush Is A Terrorist. Since I Had Not Yet Seen Every Terrorist In The World, My Sole Mistake Was In Naming Him The Greatest Of Them All. In My Opinion, He Deserves The Moniker Since He Started A War With Iraq For No Good Reason And With Malicious Intent, Killing Thousands Of American Soldiers And Hundreds Of Thousands Of Iraqis, The Vast Majority Of Whom Were Innocent Civilians. The Bush Administration Called The Deaths Of Thousands Of Civilians "Collateral Damage," A Word That Really Pisses Me Off. Collateral Damage Seems Like An Obvious Excuse To Justify Atrocities Against Civilians.

Coretta Scott King's Death At Age 78, From Respiratory Difficulties, Several Strokes, And Ovarian Cancer, Occurred Only Days After I Returned From Venezuela. I Felt A Wide Range Of Emotions In Response To That Devastating News.

I No Longer Felt As Close To Coretta And Her Kids As I Once Did. I Had Voluntarily Stepped Down As Director Of The King Center, And While The Kids Still Called Me "Uncle Harry" During Our Occasional Phone Chats, I Seldom Saw Them. Because Of My Long And Close Relationship With The Family, I Wasn't Shocked To Be Invited To Deliver A Eulogy At Coretta's Funeral. However, A Few Days Later, I Received A Phone From Mrs. King's Office Telling Me That I Would Not Be Speaking, And I Was Rather Taken Aback By This News. Moreover, I Sensed That It Would Be For The Best If I Did Not Show There At All.

After I Came Out Of My First Shock, I Contacted Martin Iii To Find Out What Had Occurred. He Apologized For

Everything. The Nephew Said To His Uncle, "Oh, Uncle Harry, There's Such Confusion Down Here," Referring To Lithonia, Georgia, Where The Burial Was To Take Place. He Seemed As Though The Whole Incident Was Beyond His Control When He Said, "Nothing Is Being Coordinated Right—I'm So Sorry About This." Not At All. To Be Honest, I Already Knew That.

Bernice, Martin's Youngest Child, Has Been Leaning More Rightward On Political Issues For Some Time. She Had Made A Public Statement Supporting Bush's Iraq Policy. She Was Also Strongly Anti-Gay, Which Brought Her Into Alliance With The Black Megachurch Pastor Eddie Long Of New Birth Missionary Baptist, Where Coretta's Burial Would Be Held. Long Adopted Bernice, And He Presented Her To His Coworkers, Including Jerry Falwell. In This Group, Right-Wing Conservative Family Values Triumphed Over Resentment, Politics, And Religious Zeal. However, Not Always Were They Successful; In September 2010, The Reverend Eddie Long Was Sued For Many Counts Of Sexual Assault Against Young Male Members Of His Flock.

As Far As Bernice Was Concerned, I Was The One Awash In Immorality Back At The Beginning Of 2006. The National Press Has Picked Up On My Recent Remarks On Hugo Chávez And George W. Bush. I Wasn't Surprised To Learn That Bernice And The Other Born-Again Types Were Upset With Them. My Worst Fears Were Realized When I Heard That The President Had Finally Consented To Attend The Ceremony. The Kids Had Made Up Their Minds Quickly When Given The Choice Between One Of Their Dad's Closest Friends And A President Their Pops Would Have Hated.

Perhaps Others In Attendance Questioned Why Reverend Long's Church Was Being Used For The Event.

Why Not Visit The Church That Marked The Beginning Of Martin And Coretta's Historic Trip, Ebenezer Baptist? One Of The Most Respected Black Personalities On The Evangelical Right, Reverend Long Received Millions Of Dollars In Donations From That Sector, Most Of Which Went To Republican Campaign Coffers. They Benefited Equally From Bush's Choice To Attend The Burial. It Brought Reverend Long And His Congregation Even More Notoriety On A National Scale. He And The Christian Right Probably Got The Idea To Donate More Money To The Party That Hates Gays Because Of This.

Before The Service, Word Spread That I Wasn't Invited, And I Heard From A Number Of Individuals, Including Jesse Jackson And Al Sharpton. They Basically Stated, "Jump In With Us" For Example, "And If They Cause Any Fuss, We'll Take It To The Next Level," Where "The Next Level" Is The Media. I Let Them Know How Much I Valued Their Encouragement. No Matter How Painful This Was, I Remarked, I Could Never Bring Myself To Approach Martin's Children, Particularly On The Anniversary Of Coretta's Passing. Further Discussion Led Us To The Realization That, In Keeping With The Spirit Of The Movement, We Need To Be Working Toward Reconciliation Rather Than Driving A Wedge Between Ourselves.

I Kept My Silence On This Matter. The Reverend Joseph Lowery, A Longtime Friend Of Martin's From Their Days Together In The Southern Christian Leadership Conference, Stole The Show With His Fiery Rhetoric And Blunt Statement That No Weapons Of Mass Destruction Had Been Found In Iraq, As I Saw On Television, Along With President And Mrs. Bush And Former Presidents Bill Clinton, George H. W. Bush, And Jimmy Carter. The Author Maya Angelou Touched Me Deeply With Her

Courteous Mention To My Absence. She Said That She Was There Representing The Millions Of People That Coretta Had Inspired But Who Were Unable To Attend The Event. She Counted Me As One Of Those People. I Was Sad That I Couldn't Attend, But Not That Sad. The Youngsters Had Matured Into Who They Now Were. What I Was, Was Myself. They Were Partly True; At This Location, We Didn't Have Much To Say To One Another. This Is A Fact That Makes Me Feel Terrible. Even More So After The Unexpected Death Of Yolanda, The Oldest Child, Who Left Behind A Vow That We Will Reunite.

The Strained State Of My Relationships With Martin's Relatives Is Bothersome, But Not Devastating. I Am No Longer Easily Derailed By Situations That Formerly May Have Done So. I Owe A Lot Of That Success To Pam. I Am Too Content With My Present Existence With Her To Bemoan My Past. With Pam, I Have Experienced The Kind Of Unconditional Love And Trust That Have Eluded Me In The Past. Many Tangled Emotional And Mental Knots Have Been Untied, I Know This To Be True. I Still Don't Understand Why, Even After So Many Years, Love Seems So Effortless."

My Longtime Therapist Peter Neubauer Was Understandably Interested In Seeing The Lady Who Had Finally Helped Me Turn My Life Around, So I Took Her To See Him One Day. When He Spotted Pam, He Immediately Broke Into A Big Grin And Hugged Her. Instantaneously, He Felt Her Genuine Kindness And Compassion. He Often Informed Me That I Was His Longest-Serving Patient, Not In Terms Of Age But Of Service Years. Our Treatment Had Developed Into A Mental Connection Over The Years. Even Though My Mental Journey Was Not Yet Complete, I Believe He Saw That I Had Gone A Long Way From The Bitter And Angry

Guy I Had Been. Pam Was The Evidence; It Was Only After I Had Resolved Many Of My Problems With Peter That I Was Ready To Receive Pam's Love With An Open Heart. Only Then Would I Be Able To Fully Trust Another Person.

It's Hard To Put Into Words The Impact Peter Had On My Life. For Fifty Years, I Had Spoken To Him Weekly, Often Several Times Each Week. He Was The Only One Except Julie And Pam Who Really Understood Me. Our Conversation Was Candid, Energetic, And Personal. Sometimes I'd Point Out To Him That His Perspective Was Colored By The Fact That He Was White Or Jewish Or Both. Sometimes The Conversation Would Get Heated, At Least On My End, But The Process Always Continued. Race Is Usually A Topic Of Discussion When A White Therapist Is Working With A Black Client. But That's Not All; We Dug A Lot Deeper Than That. I Virtually Always Waited To Consult Peter Before Making A Life-Altering Choice, Whether It Concerned My Mental Well-Being, My Relationships With My Loved Ones, Or My Creative Pursuits. When I Have A Sudden Outburst Of Rage, I Still Find Myself Wondering What Peter Might Have To Say. Peter, Though, Was Older Than Me By More Than A Decade, And I Was Shocked To Learn That At The Age Of Ninety-Four, He Was Dying.

In February Of 2008, I Paid Peter A Goodbye Visit At His Apartment, Which Was Not A Session. His Body Was Breaking Down, And As A Doctor, A Superb Doctor, He Knew Precisely What Was Happening. He Could No Longer Move Freely And His Mind Was Dulled. Without His Job, He Informed Me, He Saw No Use In Continuing To Exist. He Stated He Had Learned A Lot From Our Therapeutic Connection And Had Liked Seeing Me Improve My Relationships With Women, Children, And

The Spirits Of My Ancestors. I Got It As He Spoke And It Made Sense To Me. Finally, I Had No One But Myself To Worry About.

Later That Week, He Passed Away.

It Was A Complete Coincidence, But It Was Really Meaningful Since Pam And I Had Already Planned Our Wedding For A Few Weeks After That. We Kept It Inside The Family To Avoid The Awkward Situation Of Having To Decide Which Friends To Invite And Which To Leave Out. There Were A Whopping Thirty Individuals There, Including Grandkids, Nieces, Nephews, And In-Laws. We Both Didn't Want A Church Ceremony, So We Followed David's Lead And Had Our Wedding Reception In A Restaurant In The Big Apple. We Went To Terrace In The Sky, A Rooftop Bar With 360-Degree Views Of The City That Is Located Near Columbia University. Since Pam And I Had Already Been Living Together For Some Time, The Day We Officially Became A Couple Was A Little Anticlimactic (April 12, 2008), But It Was Still A Very Happy Day. We Decided To Have Former Mayor David Dinkins Officiate Our Wedding Since He Did Such A Wonderful Job At David's. Besides, Dave Is A Personal Buddy Of Mine. At The Drop Of A Hat, He'll Claim That I Was The One Who Ultimately Persuaded Him To Run For Mayor Of New York. I'm Still Not Sure Whether He Sees That Recommendation As A Boon Or A Bane.

When I Looked Around At Everyone At The Reunion, I Could Confidently Conclude That Everyone's Marriage Was Successful. My Children Were All Still With The People They Had Been Dating During David's Wedding, Which Was A Huge Relief. Sarafina And Amadeus, David's And Malena's Lovely Children, Were Only Eight Months Old When We Were Married.

It's Not That Nobody In The "West Coast Crowd," As Adrienne Called Them, Suffered Any Career Setbacks In The Last Eight Years; Far From It. The Two Were Still Busy Putting The Finishing Touches On Their "Packages" As Shari And Sam Described It. Shari Had Been Trying To Convince Me To Join Forces With Her For A Long Time. The Only Thing That Made Sense To Me Was When Sam Asked Me To Be In His Picture Last Supper, Which Was More Of A Stab In The Dark Than A Serious Overture. If I Accepted To Be In The Starring Role, I Would Play A Vampire, And Shari Would Produce And Direct The Film. Neither Shari Nor Sam Had Any Expectation That I Would Agree To This, Yet Here I Am. In All Honesty, It Wasn't Because I Was Dying To Be A Vampire That I Finally Consented. I Had Recently Told Myself That If Shari Ever Approached Me With Another Of Her Schemes, I Would Immediately Agree. Then They Put A Mask On Me And Hanged Me By A Harness And Pulleys For Hours Every Day. A Cross Between "The Silence Of The Lambs" And "Spider-Man: Turn Off The Dark," If You Will. I Couldn't Help But Wonder Whether Shari Was Getting Even. Even Though Principal Photography Has Wrapped, The Film Is Currently In Post-Production.

Both Gina And Scott, Who Are Now Based In Los Angeles, Are Actively Seeking Acting Parts, But Gina Has Spent The Better Part Of The Previous Several Years Producing The Documentary Sing Your Song, Which Chronicles My Participation In The Civil Rights Struggle. As The Show's West Coast Producer, She Interviewed Many Of The Participants Directly And Frequently Pushed For Things I Would Have Avoided, Including Speaking With Sidney. Some Of My Coworkers Who Sadly Died Away Soon After Being Interviewed Were Made Possible Because To Her Perseverance. Gina Is

Also A Hands-On Mom To Her Daughter Maria, Encouraging Her To Participate In School Plays And Enroll In Theatre Lessons In The Hopes That One Day Maria May Follow In Gina's Footsteps And Become An Actor. My Ancestors Still Haven't Quite Shaken The Allure Of The Stage. Despite The Difficulties, Shari And Gina Remain Committed To One Other.

David Is The Only One Of My Kids That Has Ever Been Willing To Try Anything Completely New. He Embarked On A Creative Endeavor By Founding Belafonte Arts And Media. During The Recession, He Suffered Along With The Rest Of The Banking Industry. As I Write This, David And I Are Hard At Work On A Cultural Excursion For The Service Employees International Union (Seiu) Called Bread And Roses. Its Goal Is To Inspire The Union's Over Two Million Members To Use The Arts As A Means Of Self-Expression And Cultural Preservation By Performing Or Creating Original Works Of Music, Theater, Or Literature. In Order To Get The True Tales Of Union Workers Heard By The Rest Of The Nation, We Want To See Them Set To Lyrics And Song. Their Very Own Record Label Is In The Works. There Hasn't Been A Forum Like That For Working Folks In Quite Some Time. Not Since Woody Guthrie And The Great Depression, When President Roosevelt And His Works Progress Administration Program Sparked The Great American Cultural Renaissance, Has Art Been Allowed To Flourish To Its Full Potential.

This Project With David Is All I Can Think About. More Than Forty Years Ago, The Union Established Its Bread And Roses Program At Its New York Headquarters, Which Is Located In The Middle Of Manhattan's Theatrical Area.

I Am Surrounded By A Diaspora Of African Employees Every Time I Enter The Building On My Way To The Workplace. They, Along With Their Latino And Asian Peers, Fill The Elevator With Laughter And Smiles As They Recount Their First Memories. I Am Impressed By The Hard Work Ethic Of These Employees. They Do Everything From Caring For The Sick And Crippled To Changing Bedsheets And Urinals To Raising Families. They Resemble My Mum In Many Ways And Do Many Of The Same Things. I Can Appreciate Their Predicament And Hardship. The Respect For Their Inherent Worth Is Something I Share. Our Goal In Creating Bread And Roses Is To Reflect Their Accomplishments And Celebrate Their Goals. I'm Reminded Of Something Woody Wrote In The Midst Of The Power Elite's Harsh And Devastating Attacks On American Workers:

I Was Strolling Along And Saw A Sign.
As For The Sign, It Simply Said, "No Trespassing."
However, There Was Silence On The Other Side.
You And I Were Meant To Share That Part....
In The City's Public Plazas,
Under The Wing Of A Church Tower,
I Had Located My Folks Near The Relief Office.
They Were Starving While They Waited,
Standing There, I Inquired
Do You And I Belong Here?

The Difficulty We Face Is How To Safeguard The Liberties That Americans Have Fought For A Century, But Which Are Now In Perilous Risk Of Being Lost, As Working-Class Artists Come To Embrace Our Efforts And Translate Their Labor Difficulties Into Tale And Song. As In Previous Eras, Today's Artists Have The Power To Effect Positive Change In The World. Paul Robeson Once Said, "Artists Are The Gatekeepers Of Truth And The True

Documentarians Of History," And If We Put Our Talents To Good Use, We'll Prove Him Right. I Plan To Devote The Rest Of My Life To This Endeavor.

I Have Zero Complaints About My Own Life. Concerns About What The Movement Hasn't Accomplished And How Few People Are Still Involved In The Movement Make Me Anxious About The State Of Race And Poverty In Our Nation.

Those Requirements Have Been Met To A Certain Extent, Surprisingly Enough, Since We Have A Black President. When The Civil Rights Movement First Began, Few People Ever Thought That This Day Would Arrive. It's An Incredible Demonstration Of How Far American Society Has Come In Its Acceptance Of People Of Different Races, And If Race Wasn't The Biggest Factor In The Election, Then It's Even More Remarkable That Barack Obama Was Able To Win Despite The Fact That He Isn't White. A Presidential Candidate's Race Or Gender May Not Be An Issue For Voters In The Future, Maybe In My Children's Or Their Children's Lives.

Most People Of Color In The United States Still Appear To Be Dealing With The Same Severe And Pervasive Issues They Had Fifty Years Ago. At The Time Of This Writing, Our President Has Not Even Admitted That This Is A Problem For Him, Much Less Presented A Plan Of Action That Would Motivate The American People To Get Involved And Make The Necessary Sacrifices For The Sake Of The Country.

I've Always Felt A Spiritual Core In The Politicians I've Looked Up To. Bobby Kennedy Was Sometimes Ruthlessly Pragmatic, But When Faced With Abject Poverty, He Couldn't Look Away. He Had To Speak Out About What He'd Witnessed, And When I Heard Him Speak, I Knew He Was Speaking From His Moral Core,

The Place Martin Luther King Had Advised Us To Discover. Bobby's Words Were Genuine. Nothing Can Take Its Place In This Regard.

Barack Obama May Be Charismatic And Brilliant, But He Lacks A Basic Empathy For The Downtrodden Of Any Race. The First Black President, I Imagined, Would Do All In His Power To Improve The Lives Of Black People In America's Inner Cities. The Passage Of The Stimulus Package Is Very Much Appreciated By Me. A Universal Health Insurance Law Would Be Beneficial For All Of Us, I Get That. One In Three Black Men In The United States Is In Jail, And We Have The Greatest Prison Population In The World; Still, I Keep Asking Why He Hasn't Utilized His Influence To Make The Justice System More Humane. I Want Him To State More Emphatically That There Are Racial Issues Now. Put Some Emotion Into Your Performance. He Has Effectively Abandoned The Poor By Moving To The Middle Of Politics And Away From The Left. After All, Who Else Except The Left Defends The Poor?

It's Going To Become A Lot Tougher For America's Poor. Since He Is, After All, A Realistic Leader, Our Black President Seems To Be Biting His Tongue. After More Than Half A Century In The Movement, However, I Can Say With Confidence That The Poor Will Not Just Give Up And Die, No Matter How Much The Current Political Majority May Desire Otherwise. When You're Starving, You'll Do Just About Everything To Satisfy Your Appetite. One Either Marches, Steals, Or Arms Oneself.

Race, As Anticipated By W.E.B. Du Bois In His Book Black Reconstruction In America, Dominated Discussions Throughout The Twentieth Century. When One Considers The Holocaust As An Act Of Genocide Committed By A Delusional "Superior Race" Determined

To Rid The Globe Of "Inferior" Jews (And Blacks), I Have To Agree With Him. There Is Little Question In My Mind That Race Will Continue To Rule Not Just The United States But The Whole Planet In The Twenty-First Century.

I Will Concede That Racial Progress Has Been Accomplished In The United States. Even Though America Elected Its First Black President In 2008, It Now Openly Tolerates Racial Insults And Jokes. Black Americans Make Up A Sizable Portion Of The Country's Middle Class. Southern Racists' Worst Nightmare Is Coming True: As More And More People Of Different Races Marry One Other, Race Becomes Less Of An Issue In The Workplace. That's All Positive. My Disappointment Lies In The Apparent Lack Of Heirs. Where Are The Young, Radical Activists Who Challenge The Status Quo? They May Be Found In Egypt, Tunisia, And Other Openly Repressive Countries. Contrarily, Such Is Not The Case Here.

The Exceedingly Wealthy At The Top, And Everyone Else Below Them. And Rather Than Trying To Bring That System Down, The Following Generation Is Aiming For The Pinnacle Of Success Inside It. How Well-Oiled Is The Machine That Keeps Oppressing, So Well-Oiled That Those Who Could Fight It Are Co-Opted, Their Fury Is Drained, And Their Greed Is Amplified Until Those Who Have Been Squeezed The Hardest By The Two-Tier System Have Nothing Left To Lose And Take Their Frustrations Out On The Streets.

Mlk Famously Observed That Rage Was A Key Component In The Recipe For Progress. And I Agree Wholeheartedly With It. As You Might Imagine, I Made An Angry First Impression On Him. My Anger Had Served As A Shield. Martin Saw The Merit In My Frustration. But

Our Cause Taught Me How To Channel That Energy Into Something Useful.

Two Little Beings From An Uncharted Alien Planet Have Just Entered My Life, And They Have Changed It In Profound Ways. Mateo And Oliive Are Pam's Grandkids. To Me, These Are Wonders Worth Celebrating, Seeing, And Seeing Again. Adrienne, Shari, David, And Gina; Rachel, Brian, Maria, Sarafina, And Amadeus; And The First Two Great-Grandchildren, Isabella And Gabriel, All Entered My Life At Different Points In My Journey. These Eleven Children Are The Extensions Of My Gene Pool. As I See These Youngsters Dive Headfirst Into The World Around Them, Pulled By The Allure Of Cutting-Edge Technology, I Can't Help But Feel Both Concerned About And Jealous Of Them. I'm Concerned Because Modern Technologies Don't Appear To Bring Us Closer Together But Rather Drive Us Farther Away. Jealousy, Since Everything This New World Has To Offer Should Help Us Reach The Loftier Goals We've Been Working For.

My Experience Was Very Unforgettable. I'm Well Aware That We're Living In A Brutal And Destructive Society, Where People Are Losing Their Moral Compass And Their Ability To See Beyond The Mundane. Still, I Have To Hold On To The Hope That Our Finest Days Are Ahead Of Us, And That We Will Find Solace In One Another Along The Road.

I Wrote That Tune!

Chapter 7

Harry Belafonte Is An Iconic American Singer, Composer, Actor, And Activist Who Has Significantly Impacted The Field Of Music During His Career. He Was Born In The United States. He Is Well-Known For His One-Of-A-Kind And Varied Musical Style, Which Takes Influence From A Wide Range Of Musical Subgenres Including Calypso, Jazz, Folk Music, And Blues. His Career As A Musician Spans Many Decades, And He Has Recorded More Than 30 Cds During The Course Of His Career.

Early Years As Well As Influences From The Musical World

On March 1, 1927, Harry Belafonte Was Born In Harlem, New York. He Was An American Singer And Actor. He Was Born Into Poverty And Had To Overcome A Great Deal Of Adversity Throughout His Life. Despite This, He Has Always Had A Strong Affinity For Music, Which He Attributes To The Fact That His Mother Was A Musician And Sung In The Choir At Their Local Church. The Likes Of Louis Armstrong, Duke Ellington, And Nat King Cole Were Among The Musicians Who Had A Significant Impact On Belafonte's Musical Development.

The Beginning Of Belafonte's Career

The Early 1950s Marked The Beginning Of Belafonte's Career As A Musician. In The Beginning, He Established Himself As A Musician By Playing In The More Intimate Settings Of New York City's Pubs And Clubs. Soon After, He Attracted The Notice Of Those Working In The Music Business, And In 1952, Rca Victor Records Offered Him A Recording Deal.

His Debut Album, Titled "Mark Twain And Other Folk Favorites," Was Published In 1954. It Included A Variety Of Folk Songs And Spirituals On Its Track Listing. The Record Was Met With Widespread Praise And Was Instrumental In Launching Belafonte Into A More Prominent Position Within The Music Business.

The Crucial Role Of Calypso In One's Early Career
The Album "Calypso," Which Contained Belafonte's Recognizable Style Of Music, Was The Artist's Breakthrough Work And Was Published In 1956. It Was The First Album In History To Sell More Than One Million Copies Due To The Enormous Popularity Of The Record. The Album Includes The Hit Songs "Day-O (The Banana Boat Song)" And "Jamaica Farewell," Which Helped To Promote Calypso Music In The United States As Well As In Other Countries Across The Globe.

The Success That Belafonte Had With "Calypso" Led To A String Of Albums And Tours That Were Also Very Popular During The 1950s And 1960s. He Became A Well-Known Figure And Was Widely Considered To Be One Of The Most Successful And Influential Artists Of His Day. He Was An Active Participant In The Civil Rights Struggle, The Anti-Apartheid Campaign, And Other Humanitarian Initiatives, And He Made Use Of His Reputation To Advocate For Many Social And Political Issues.

Various Forms Of Musical Cooperation And Productions
Throughout His Career, Belafonte Not Only Performed Solo But Also Worked With A Variety Of Different Artists. Miriam Makeba, The Chad Mitchell Trio, And The Belafonte Folk Singers Are Just A Few Of The Artists That He Collaborated With Over His Career. Additionally, He

Has Released Albums In A Number Of Other Languages, Including French, German, And Spanish.

Additionally, Belafonte Was Well-Known For His Work In Both The Cinema And Television Industries. Throughout The Course Of His Career, He Had Roles In A Number Of Films And Television Series, Some Of The Most Notable Of Which Are "Carmen Jones," "Island In The Sun," And "The Banana Boat Song." In The Late 1960s, He Was Also The Host Of His Own Television Variety Program Called "The Harry Belafonte Show."

Legacy And Repercussions
The Body Of Work That Harry Belafonte Has Produced As A Musician Has Had A Substantial Influence Not Just On The Field Of Music But Also On Society As A Whole. His Music Was Instrumental In The Spread Of Calypso Music Across The United States And The Rest Of The Globe, And He Used His Celebrity To Advocate For Social And Political Topics That He Felt Strongly About. He Was A Significant Player In The Civil Rights Movement, The Anti-Apartheid Struggle, And Other Humanitarian Endeavors, And During His Career, He Has Been Honored With A Great Deal Of Recognition, Including A Number Of Prizes And Honours.

Chapter 8

Not Only Was Harry Belafonte A Well-Known Musician And Activist, But He Also Had A Successful Acting Career And Was A Well-Known Television Personality. His Work In The Realm Of Television Spans Many Decades And Includes A Diverse Array Of Roles, Ranging From The Presenter Of His Own Variety Program To Appearances In Both Dramatic And Comedic Television Series. In This Piece, We Will Investigate Harry Belafonte's Career In Television In Great Detail, Talking About His Most Famous Projects, Successes, And The Influence He Had On The Business.

Appearances On Television In Their Infancy
In 1953, Harry Belafonte Made His Debut On Television By Appearing On "The Ed Sullivan Show." He Gave A Performance Of His Smash Hit "Matilda," And He Was An Immediate Success. Audiences Were Captivated By His Charming Demeanor And Distinctive Style Of Music. This Performance Was Essential In Kicking Off Belafonte's Career And Laying The Groundwork For His Subsequent Achievements In The Field Of Television.

In The Years That Followed, Belafonte Appeared On A Number Of Other Television Shows, Such As "The Dinah Shore Chevy Show," "The Colgate Comedy Hour," And "The Perry Como Show." These Performances Served To Further Solidify Belafonte's Status As A Rising Star In The Entertainment Business And Helped To Broaden His Audience Outside The Realm Of Music. In Addition, These Appearances Helped To Bring In New Fans.

The Show Starring Harry Belafonte

In 1960, Harry Belafonte Made History By Being The First Person Of African Descent To Host His Own Television Variety Show. His Program Was Titled "The Harry Belafonte Show." The Program Highlighted Belafonte's Abilities As A Performer And Entertainer By Including A Variety Of Segments, Including Music, Comedy, And Interviews With Famous People. Additionally, It Contributed To The Dismantling Of Racial Barriers In The Entertainment Business, Making Way For Subsequent Generations Of Black Singers And Opening Doors Of Opportunity For Them.

The "Harry Belafonte Show" Was A Revolutionary Show That Expanded The Bounds Of What Was Possible On Television At The Time. The Program Is Credited With Helping To Create The Modern Television Industry. It Included Performances By Some Of The Most Well-Known Personalities In The Music Industry, Such As Bob Dylan, Lena Horne, And Stevie Wonder, And It Contributed To The Promotion Of Racial Equality And Social Justice By The Material That It Presented.

Even Though The Program Was Only On The Air For A Single Season, It Had A Profound Effect Not Just On The Business But Also On American Society As A Whole. It Served To Usher In A New Age Of Diversity And Representation On Television, Setting The Way For Numerous Series That Would Follow In Its Footsteps In The Years That Would Come After It.

Additional Roles On Television
Throughout His Career, Harry Belafonte Participated On A Number Of Different Television Shows In Addition To Presenting His Own Variety Show. During This Time, He

Also Hosted His Own Show. He Played The Character Of Frank Mosca In The 1980s Drama "Miami Vice," And His Appearances On The Show Were Recurrent. He Has Had Guest Appearances On Episodes Of "The Love Boat," "The Cosby Show," And "The Muppet Show."

However, Acting And Hosting Were Not The Only Things That Belafonte Did On Television Throughout His Career. In Addition To This, He Was Featured In A Number Of Documentaries And Other Non-Fiction Shows, In Which He Used His Celebrity Status To Advocate For Various Political And Social Concerns. One Of His Most Prominent Documentary Appearances Was In The 1974 Children's Show "Free To Be... You And Me," Which Encouraged Gender Equality And Diversity. He Appeared In The Program.

Resulting Effects On The Industry
The Contributions That Harry Belafonte Made To The Field Of Television Have Had A Long-Lasting Influence On Both The Business As A Whole And On American Society More Generally. The Ground-Breaking Work That He Did As The Host Of "The Harry Belafonte Show" Contributed To The Dismantling Of Racial Barriers, As Well As The Promotion Of Diversity And Representation On Television. In Addition To This, He Made Use Of His Prominence To Advocate For Other Political And Social Causes, Helping To Bring Attention To Topics Such As Civil Rights, Apartheid, And The Need For Nuclear Disarmament.

The Impact That Belafonte Had On The Television Business Is Still Being Felt In The Current Day, As Presenters And Producers Continue To Advocate For

More Racial And Ethnic Variety In The Programming They Produce. His Legacy As A Pioneer And A Champion For Social Justice Has Inspired An Endless Number Of Individuals To Utilize Their Platforms To Affect Good Change In The World. He Was A Trailblazer.

Chapter 9

Harry Belafonte, An American Singer, Actor, And Civil And Human Rights Campaigner, Passed Away On Tuesday Due To Congestive Heart Failure At 96. In A Manner That Made People All Around The Globe Listen, He Overcame Racial Boundaries While Striking A Balance Between His Advocacy And His Artistic Endeavors. The Death Of Belafonte, Who Had Won Emmys, Grammys, Oscars, And Tonys Over His Career, Took Place At His Home In New York, According To An Announcement Made By His Publicist. He Died On April 25, 2023, In Manhattan, New York, United States

Printed in Poland
by Amazon Fulfillment
Poland Sp. z o.o., Wrocław
02 May 2023

42232628-c434-4fe5-84d2-4b6fe70cfda0R01